iMovie™ 2

fast&easy®

Check the Web for Updates

To check for updates or corrections relevant to this book and/or CD-ROM visit our updates page on the Web at **http://www.prima-tech.com/updates**.

Send Us Your Comments

To comment on this book or any other PRIMA TECH title, visit our reader response page on the Web at **http://www.prima-tech.com/comments**.

How to Order

For information on quantity discounts, contact the publisher: Prima Publishing, P.O. Box 1260BK, Rocklin, CA 95677-1260; (916)787-7000. On your letterhead, include information concerning the intended use of the books and the number of books you wish to purchase.

iMovie™ 2
fast&easy®

Kevin Harreld

A DIVISION OF PRIMA PUBLISHING

A Division of Prima Publishing

Prima Publishing, colophon, and Fast & Easy are registered trademarks of Prima Communications, Inc. PRIMA TECH is a trademark of Prima Communications, Inc., Roseville, California 95661.

Publisher: Stacy L. Hiquet
Associate Marketing Manager: Heather Buzzingham
Managing Editor: Sandy Doell
Acquisitions Editor: Lynette Quinn
Project Editor: Cathleen D. Snyder
Technical Reviewer: Mark Loper
Copy Editor: Cindy Kogut
Interior Layout: Marian Hartsough Associates
Cover Design: Prima Design Team
Indexer: Johnna Dinse
Proofreader: Kelli Crump

ISBN: 0-7615-3467-9
Library of Congress Catalog Card Number: 00-110731
Printed in the United States of America

00 01 02 03 04 DD 10 9 8 7 6 5 4 3 2 1

To Lisa and Genevieve,

always my Best Actresses;

and Best Actor, Jackson,

the newest focus of my feature presentations

Acknowledgments

Special thanks go to Stacy Hiquet and Lynette Quinn for taking me seriously when I said I could do another book. Thanks also to Ben Dominitz and Matt Carleson for always having respect and confidence in me. Prima is a wonderful company to work for. Thanks also to rookie-no-more Cathleen Snyder, who managed the sequel flawlessly, and to Cindy Kogut and Mark Loper for their quality insight. Kudos also to Kelli Crump, my first mentor in book publishing (and proofreader of this book), and Bill Mishler, my Zen master. Final thanks to my parents for always being there for me . . . and for buying me a camera.

About the Author

KEVIN HARRELD is an Acquisitions Editor for the Tech Division of Prima Publishing. After years of working behind the scenes, editing numerous Tech books, he took a starring role as author of *iMovie Fast & Easy*. The box office success of the first book (or maybe it was Apple's decision to release iMovie 2) pushed him to pen the sequel, *iMovie 2 Fast & Easy*. Before book writing and editing, Kevin also worked for several years in roles in the newspaper industry, where he learned the definition of deadline. Spending a year as a film studies minor, living in movie houses and video stores (before he had kids), and listening to Joe Bob Briggs has made Kevin believe he's an authority on movies. Kevin lives in Indianapolis with his wife Lisa, daughter Genevieve, son Jackson, and hound Dignan. He enjoys fairways and greens, hardwoods and diamonds, and big screens and artificial butter flavor.

Contents at a Glance

PART IV
IMOVIE 2 EXTRAS 199

PART V
APPENDIXES 287

Contents

PART II
THE IMPORTING AND EDITING ROOM. 23

Introduction

So, you wanna be in pictures? Home movie Hitchcock wannabes now have a simple and exciting desktop video-editing tool: Apple's iMovie 2. iMovie 2 is the perfect tool for turning those long, boring home videos into interesting, polished productions that your family and friends will enjoy. Let's face it, without video-editing software to sharpen your home movies, even your own kids and creative filming techniques (of the floor) can be dull.

With iMovie 2, you can be a modern day Orson Welles and write, direct, and star in your own original short films, or edit those shelves of dusty, unwatchable video tapes you've had for years. You've probably seen better film on teeth. After you master iMovie 2, you will start to think like a movie director or editing room technician every time you pick up the camera.

iMovie 2 Fast & Easy will teach you to make better home movies using Apple's exciting video-editing software. You will learn to edit your video clips, add smooth transitions between clips, insert opening titles and closing credits, add soundtracks and sound effects, create special effects, and export your finished production. You'll also learn some camera shooting tricks to help you visualize a better epic. Finally, you'll learn how you can utilize features of photo manipulation programs to enhance your productions, and how to create a simple Web page to post your final masterpieces.

Prima Tech's *Fast & Easy* guides are visual solutions to getting started and learning computer-related subjects. The easy-to-follow, highly visual *Fast & Easy* style makes this a perfect learning tool. Computer terms are clearly explained in non-technical language, and numbered steps keep explanations to a minimum to help you learn faster.

Special Features of This Book

In addition to the visual and detailed descriptions of useful tasks, this book also contains some additional comments.

Notes give background and additional information about various features.

Tips reveal shortcuts or hints that make using iMovie even simpler.

A comprehensive glossary of terms is also included, as well as informative appendixes to help you download and install iMovie 2 from Apple's Web site, and to teach you some useful keyboard shortcuts. Have fun with *iMovie 2 Fast & Easy*, and good luck directing your home movies. Your family and friends will thank you.

PART I
Film School 101

1

Tools of the Trade

What tools do you need to become a desktop moviemaker? With iMovie 2 and the plummeting prices of digital video cameras, you can now afford to use state-of-the-art video and computer hardware. However, it's important to know the peripherals of iMovie 2, its computer system requirements, and the digital video cameras it supports. In this chapter, you'll learn how to:

- Identify supported digital video cameras
- Identify the computer system requirements
- Use FireWire
- Work with analog video converters

Digital Video Cameras

Apple's iMovie Web site (http://www.apple.com/imovie) lists the digital video cameras that are supported by iMovie 2. As of the writing of this book, the list includes the following:

- Sony DCR-PC1
- Sony DCR-PC10
- Sony DCR-PC100
- Sony DCR-PC2E (PAL)
- Sony DCR-PC3
- Sony DCR-TRV-5E (PAL)
- Sony DCR-TRV-8E (PAL)
- Sony DCR-TRV7
- Sony DCR-TRV8
- Sony DCR-TRV9

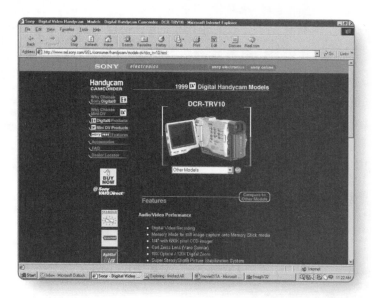

- Sony DCR-TRV11
- Sony DCR-TR7000
- Sony DCR-TRV103
- Sony DCR-TRV110
- Sony DCR-TRV310
- Sony DCR-TRV510
- Sony DCR-TRV900
- Sony DCR-TRV900e

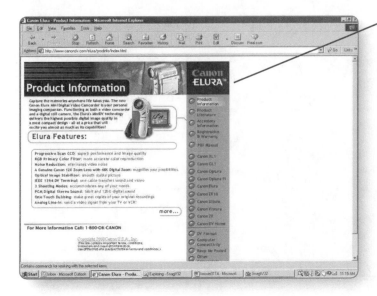

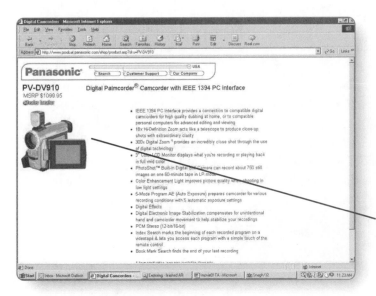

- Canon Elura
- Canon Elura2
- Canon GL1
- Canon Mini DV MV3i (PAL)
- Canon MV1 (PAL)
- Canon MV10 (PAL)
- Canon MV100 (PAL)
- Canon MV20i (PAL)
- Canon MV30i (PAL)
- Canon MV200i (PAL)
- Canon MV300i (PAL)
- Canon Optura
- Canon Optura Pi
- Canon Ultura
- Canon Vistura
- Canon XL1
- Canon XM1 (PAL)
- Canon XL1 (PAL)
- Canon ZR
- Canon ZR10
- Panasonic AG-EZ20
- Panasonic AG-EZ30
- Panasonic PV-DV710
- Panasonic PV-DV910
- Sharp VL-PD3

In this book, I use Sony's DCR-TRV510 Digital8 Handycam model. Sony's Digital8 camcorders offer a bridge between the old and the new. Basically, you can capture digital information on standard 8mm and Hi8 videotapes. This is an advantage because 8mm and Hi8 tapes are much more affordable than mini DV tapes for DV camcorder models, and because 8mm and Hi8 tapes that contain your old analog video can be played back and imported into iMovie through your Digital8 camcorder. 8mm tapes are still considered the most popular cassette format for camcorders. Sony does recommend that you use Hi8 (Metal Particle) tapes for optimum quality in capturing your digital footage.

If you have a camcorder that is not on this list, and you're not sure if it is a digital video camera, you can check with the camera manufacturer to find out. The camcorder also requires a FireWire, iLink, or IEEE 1394 port for importing and exporting video. If you aren't sure whether your camcorder has this capability, check with your camera manufacturer.

The Software and the System

By purchasing a new iMac DV, Power Mac G4, Power Mac G4 Cube, iBook, or PowerBook, you have already acquired the iMovie 2 software—it comes installed on the machines.

You can also obtain a copy of iMovie 2 for $49 (U.S.) by downloading it from the Apple Store (http://www.apple.com/store). See Appendix A, "Acquiring and Installing iMovie 2," to learn how to download and install iMovie 2.

Before you download iMovie 2, make sure your Macintosh computer has the following minimum system requirements:

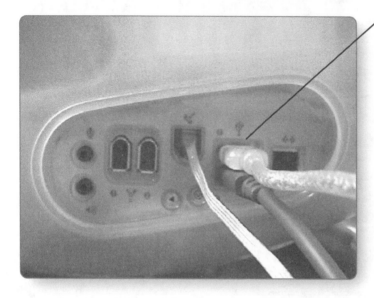

- A G3 (or later) 300 MHz (or faster) processor with a built-in FireWire port

- Mac Operating System (OS) 9.0.4 or later

- QuickTime 4.1.2 or later

- 64 MB of RAM (128 MB is recommended)

- FireWire 2.4 or later

- 4 GB of hard disk space

- A monitor capable of displaying thousands (millions recommended) of colors at a screen resolution of 800 × 600 (1024 × 768 is recommended)

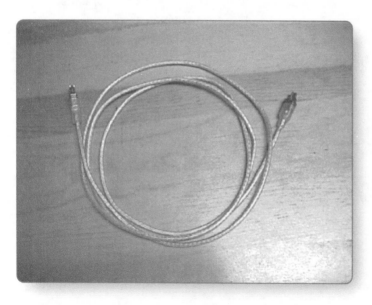

FireWire

FireWire is a multimedia peripheral that allows you to import and export video and audio from your camcorder at tremendous speeds—400 megabits per second (Mbps), to be exact. FireWire has 30 times more bandwidth than USB (*Universal Serial Bus*), which used to be the standard for this type of activity.

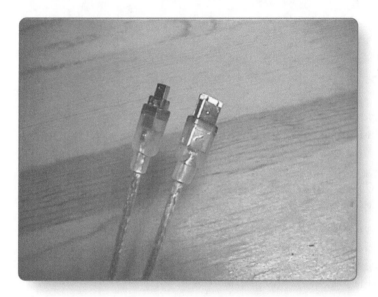

FireWire is also called iLink or IEEE 1394. The FireWire cable has four-pin and six-pin connectors to connect your digital camcorder to your Macintosh.

Analog Video Converters

iMovie is designed to work with video cameras that support digital video (DV). However, you can convert other video formats (8mm, Hi8, VHS, SVHS) to DV format by using a special converter box. Sony makes this converter box, which is available at Apple's online store (http://www.apple.com/imovie/shoot.html).

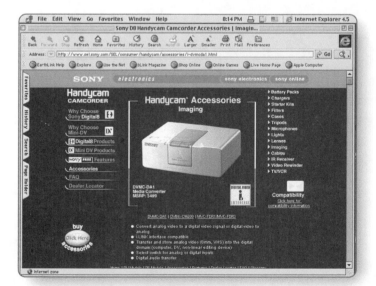

The converter box has standard S-video and RCA input/output ports for video and audio, and a FireWire input/output port. It can therefore convert analog video to a digital video signal, or digital video to analog.

You can use all the editing features of iMovie with this box, but you cannot capture video using the box. You must manually capture video, which shouldn't be a problem since you will probably be doing it in that manner anyway.

Another way to import analog video into iMovie is to dub the video onto a DV tape and then import the footage. You'll learn how to do this in Chapter 3, "Lights, Camera . . . Starting Your Epic." This solution works for those who have DV camcorders and want to import their old VHS videos (or other formats) into iMovie for editing. However, if you only have a non-DV camcorder and you want to use iMovie, you'll have to use the Sony converter box. At about $400, it's not cheap, so you might want to consider picking up a DV camcorder for a few dollars more.

2

Capturing Footage

iMovie 2 is a great editing tool, but it alone cannot help you make great movies. A great movie begins with the footage that you capture. The nice thing about this powerful editing tool is that you don't have to capture footage in chronological order—you can capture whatever you want and piece it together later. Just make sure you capture footage in a variety of angles, zooms, compositions, and so on, so you can put together an interesting video in the end. I hope that the hints in this chapter will help you piece together an Academy Award–nominated film—or at least keep your friends from falling asleep when they watch your iMovies. In this chapter, you'll learn how to:

- Capture full, medium, and close-up shots
- Improve your zooming and panning
- Vary camera angles and shot lengths
- Improve lighting
- Steady your camcorder

Moviemaking Composition Basics

Whether you are capturing video or extracting clips from existing videotapes, it's a good idea to have a picture in your mind of what you want your video to say or accomplish. You don't have to sketch out a storyboard like they do in Hollywood, but some advance thought will help you produce a more captivating finished product.

Including an Establishing Shot

The *establishing shot*, or *full shot*, shows the audience the setting of the scene and establishes how the subject of your movie fits in with the background or surroundings. You should have this shot somewhere at the beginning of your movie, so your audience can see the big picture early on.

Moving into Medium Shots

Medium shots reveal the action and subject of the movie.

They generally show one to three players within a small area, and include the gestures and expressions of the subjects in the shot.

My Close-Up, Please

Close-up shots introduce the individual players to the audience.

Expressions and emotions are revealed through zoomed-in, tight frames of your actors' faces. Close-up shots of subtle objects, such as a time clock ticking slowly away at a sporting event, are also very effective.

Shooting Better Video

Techniques such as zooming and panning add to the effectiveness of your movie, but you must use them judiciously and correctly. Here's a quick tour of the camera dos and don'ts to help you in your moviemaking.

Zooming

It takes a while to get the feel for delicately zooming in and out with your camcorder. It's important to zoom in slowly from a full shot to a close-up and out from a medium shot to a full shot. Many people make the mistake of constantly zooming in and out, thus confusing the viewers.

A better way to create the same effect might be to stop recording, move to a new location or change your zoom setting, and then start recording again. This is frequently called a *jump cut*, or a *cut zoom in/out*.

Panning

A *panning shot* rotates the video camera along a horizontal line, from right to left or vice versa. A common mistake is to quickly sweep across a scene back and forth, dizzying the viewer.

Again, a better practice is probably to stop the camcorder and vary the angles and shot lengths. Panning is effective when done slowly and steadily, however, and is useful when capturing footage of, say, the Grand Canyon.

Varying Angles and Shot Lengths

As I mentioned before, one of the most effective ways to make your movie more engaging is to vary the angles and shot lengths.

Capture or select footage from the front, side, above, and straight on. Also, use full shots, medium shots, and close-ups throughout your movies.

Lighting

Bad lighting can easily wash out your videos. This might go without saying, but try to avoid shooting into a bright light, such as sunlight, lamplight, or light blazing through a window. Try to put your main light source behind and to one side of you, so that your subject is well lit and doesn't cast any shadows.

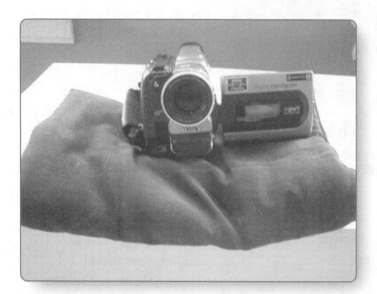

Steadying Secrets

Even though many camcorders have stabilization features that compensate for your shaky hands, it can be difficult to keep the camera still.

Tripods are the best solution for shots that absolutely need to be steady. You can also use pillows and beanbags for support. Pillows and beanbags mold to fit the contours of your camcorder while you rest it on the ground or other flat surface.

Leaning on a table to brace yourself also gives you a steadier shot. Or, you can kneel or sit down and rest the camcorder on your free knee or in your lap to reduce those camera shakes.

Other Nonstatic Shots

Most of the time, it is your subjects that should be moving, not the camera. In certain situations, though, you might find it effective to use *tracking shots*, in which you physically move along with the camera as it is shooting. Be careful, though. You still have to be very steady and avoid the nauseatingly jerky shots that this type of technique can produce. Think *Blair Witch Project*. Enough said.

Unique Angle Perspectives and Camera Tricks

Don't be afraid to experiment. The way you frame a scene, or position, group, arrange, and view your players or objects can add emotional impact to your finished production.

Tilting the camera slightly can add tension to a scene.

Use dramatic angles. Low camera angles can make your characters and objects appear tall and powerful. Diminish your characters and objects with high camera angles.

Use extreme close-ups to frame inanimate objects, as well as your characters.

Part I Review Questions

1. What video cameras are compatible with iMovie 2? *See Digital Video Cameras in Chapter 1*

2. What is digital video? *See Chapter 1*

3. What are the minimum computer system requirements to run iMovie 2? *See The Software and the System in Chapter 1*

4. Why is FireWire important to iMovie 2? *See FireWire in Chapter 1*

5. Can you use your analog video in iMovie 2? *See Analog Video Converters in Chapter 1*

6. What is an establishing shot? *See Including an Establishing Shot in Chapter 2*

7. Why is it important to limit zooming and panning with your camcorder? *See Zooming and Panning in Chapter 2*

8. What's a better way to use the effects of zooming in and out or panning back and forth? *See Varying Angles and Shot Lengths in Chapter 2*

9. What are some tricks to help you keep your camera steady during filming? *See Steadying Secrets in Chapter 2*

10. How can you avoid bad lighting? *See Lighting in Chapter 2*

PART II

The Importing and Editing Room

3

Lights, Camera . . . Starting Your Epic

Now that you know the basics about your equipment and how to capture video, it's time to fire up iMovie and feel your way around the iMovie screen. Quiet on the set, 'cause we're getting ready to roll. In this chapter, you'll learn how to:

- Connect your camcorder to your Mac
- Start iMovie
- Create a new project
- Work with the iMovie screen
- Preview your video
- Get help

Connecting Your Camcorder

The new iMac DV, Power Mac G4, Power Mac G4 Cube, iBook, and PowerBook come with the FireWire cable you need to connect your digital video camera to your computer. Two FireWire ports are built into these machines. If you aren't using an iMac DV, Power Mac G4, Power Mac G4 Cube, iBook, or PowerBook, your older Macintosh machine must have a built-in FireWire port or an add-on FireWire card for you to be able to connect to your DV camera and import digital video footage.

NOTE

If all you plan to do is edit digital video, QuickTime movies, or still pictures in iMovie 2, you don't need a FireWire port and cable. You can download, install, and run iMovie 2 on Macintosh computers that meet the minimum system requirements; you just can't import digital video from your camcorder.

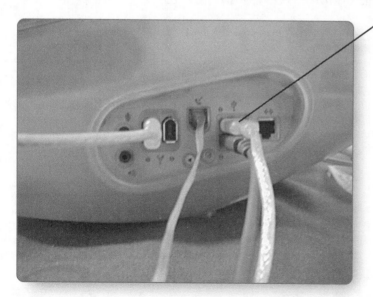

Plug the longer, flatter (six-pin) end of the FireWire cable into the appropriate port in your Mac . . .

. . . and the smaller, square (four-pin) end into the appropriate slot in your camcorder. The position of the appropriate camcorder slot will vary depending on the make and model of your camera. Now you're ready to roll.

Opening iMovie for the First Time

If iMovie 2 is already installed on your computer, all you have to do is fire it up from the icon on your desktop or in the iMovie folder on your hard drive. If you still need to acquire and install iMovie 2 from Apple, refer to Appendix A, "Acquiring and Installing iMovie 2."

Starting iMovie from the Desktop

If you have the preinstalled iMovie 2 program on your machine or have successfully acquired and installed iMovie 2 from Apple, you can simply start iMovie from the desktop.

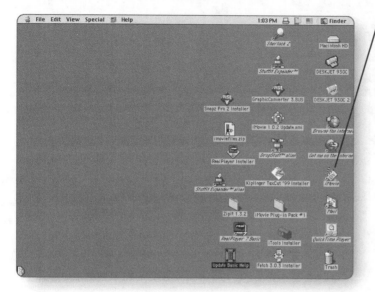

1. Double-click on the **iMovie icon** on your desktop. The program will start. A QuickTime movie will open and offer you four options: New Project, Open Project, Open Tutorial, and Quit.

2. Click on **one** of the following options:

- **New Project**. This will allow you to create a new iMovie project. You will learn more about opening a new project in the "Creating a New Project" section later in this chapter.

- **Open Project**. This will allow you to open an existing iMovie project that you have already created. If this is the first time you've used iMovie, you obviously will not have any existing iMovie projects to open. You will learn how to open an existing iMovie project in Chapter 4, "Importing Footage," after you have had a chance to import footage and create some movies.

- **Open Tutorial**. This will allow you to open the iMovie tutorial project. The tutorial has sample video clips of a dog-washing venture by a couple of youngsters. You can practice editing techniques with this sample footage before diving into your own videos. You can learn more about the tutorial in the "Running the Help Tutorial" section later in this chapter.

- **Quit**. This will allow you to exit iMovie.

Starting iMovie from the Folder

You can also open iMovie from its folder on your Macintosh hard drive (HD).

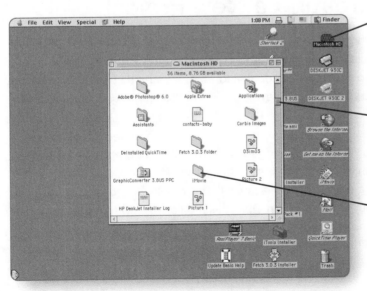

1. Double-click on the **Macintosh hard drive icon** on your desktop. The hard drive window will open.

2. Press and hold the **mouse button** on the scroll bar and **drag** the **scroll bar** up or down to search for the iMovie folder.

3. Double-click on the **iMovie folder**. The iMovie folder will open.

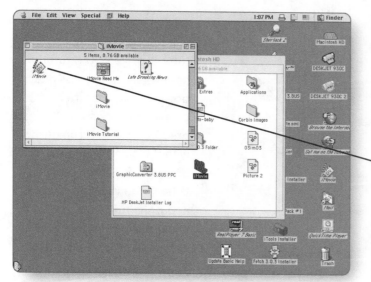

NOTE

More than likely your iMovie folder will reside in your Macintosh HD folder, but the location might vary.

4. Double-click on the **iMovie icon.** The iMovie program will begin. Again, if this is the first time you have started iMovie 2, a QuickTime movie will open and offer you four options: New Project, Open Project, Open Tutorial, and Quit (see the "Starting iMovie from the Desktop," section earlier in this chapter).

Creating a New Project

When you start iMovie for the first time, a QuickTime movie will play and give you four options: New Project, Open Project, Open Tutorial, and Quit. If you are still at this opening screen, click on New Project and then jump to Step 3 in this section.

The default opening QuickTime movie only appears when you run iMovie for the first time. Once you choose to create a new project or open the tutorial, this movie will no longer show up (but, if you click on Quit, this movie *will* appear again the next time you open iMovie). The next time you open iMovie, you will see the last iMovie project on which you worked. In that case, follow these steps to create a new iMovie project.

1. **Click** on **File**. The File menu will appear.

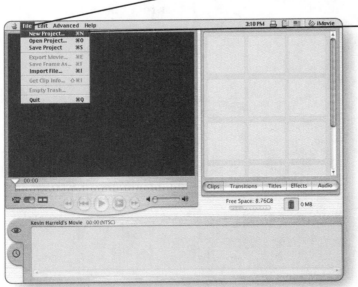

2. **Click** on **New Project**. The Create New Project dialog box will open.

3. **Click** in the **Name text box** and **type** a **file name** for your movie.

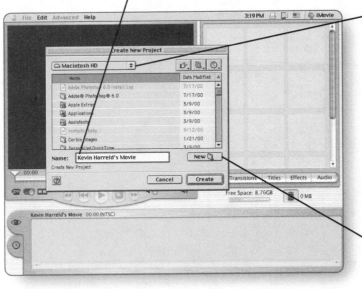

4. **Click and hold** the **mouse button** on the up and down arrows to select a destination for a folder in which you will store your iMovie project. A few choices will appear, including Macintosh HD and Desktop.

5. **Choose** a **destination** and **release** the **mouse button**. The destination will be selected.

6. **Click** on the **New Folder button**. The New Folder message box will appear.

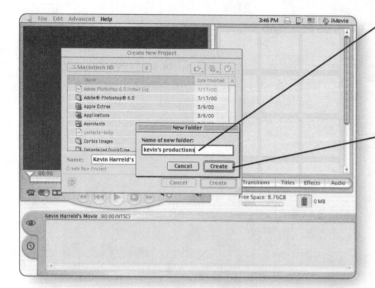

7. Click in the **Name of new folder text box** and **type** a **name** for your folder. You can use this folder to organize and keep track of all your epics.

8. Click on **Create**. The Create New Project dialog box will open, with your folder title in the destination list at the top and your movie file name in the Name text box.

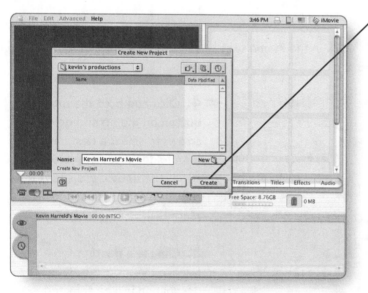

9. Click on **Create**.

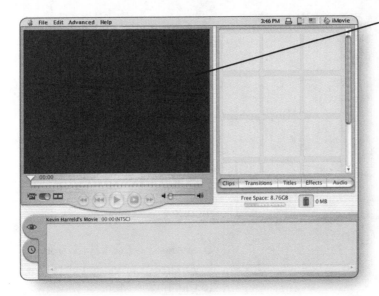

The iMovie screen will open with a blank Monitor window and your movie file name in the Clip Viewer at the bottom of the screen.

Previewing Your Video in the Monitor Window

You can start previewing your footage with just a click of your mouse button. Make sure your camera is switched to VTR/VCR mode, or you won't be able to see your footage on your computer screen.

1. Click on the **Play button**. Your video will play in the Monitor window.

2. Click on the **Rewind and Fast Forward buttons** to scan through your video. Your video will rewind or fast forward in the direction you chose.

TIP

You can use the Rewind and Fast Forward buttons on your camcorder to achieve the same results.

3. Click on the **Pause button** to pause your video, or the **Play button** again to stop playing your video. Your video will pause or stop, depending on which option you selected.

4. Click on the **Play Full-Screen button**. Your video will play full-screen on your computer's monitor.

5. Press the **Esc key** on your keyboard. Your video will return to the iMovie Monitor window.

NOTE

The video playback on your monitor will be choppier than the playback you see on the viewfinder or flip-screen of your camcorder. This is because digital video on your computer monitor only plays at approximately 20 frames per second. Normal DV plays at about 30 frames per second.

What's on the iMovie Screen?

Now that you've started iMovie, you will want to know all of the fabulous features you can toy with to make the perfect production.

Here's a quick tour around the iMovie screen:

- **Monitor window**. This is where you can preview your video directly from your digital camera, using the Rewind, Fast Forward, Play, Play Full-Screen, and Pause buttons along the bottom of the window. You will also preview your clips and iMovies here.

- **Scrolling Shelf**. This is where you'll store clips that you might decide to use later on in your final epic.

- **Design panels**. This is where you'll go to enhance your movies with titles, transitions, audio, and special effects.

- **Trash**. This is where you can discard your unwanted clips and free up that valuable hard disk space.

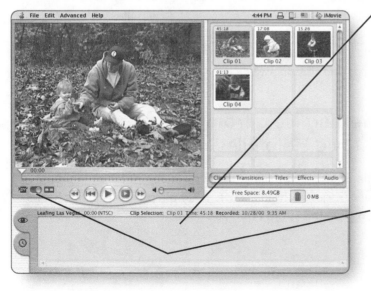

- **Timeline**. This is where your movie will come together. You will edit, place, and arrange clips and transitions by clicking on the Clip Viewer tab (the eye icon), and you'll edit, place, and arrange sound by clicking on the Timeline Viewer tab (the clock icon).

- **Mode button**. You can click on this to use Camera mode (for transferring video from a camcorder) or Edit mode (for editing your movie).

Menu bar. As usual, the File, Edit, and Help menus guide you through tasks.

Disk space gauge. You can use this feature to monitor your available hard disk space.

You will learn how to use all of these features in much more detail in the subsequent chapters of this book.

Getting Help

If you run into trouble and need a quick solution to your problem, you can always access the Help files within iMovie. If I've done my job, by the time you finish reading this book you'll never need to open these Help features. But, I've never been one to turn away a helping hand.

Getting Help from the iMovie Help Files

The iMovie Help files offer a way to search for answers to specific questions in iMovie. A simple point, click, and search can yield the information you need.

1. **Click** on **Help**. The Help menu will appear.

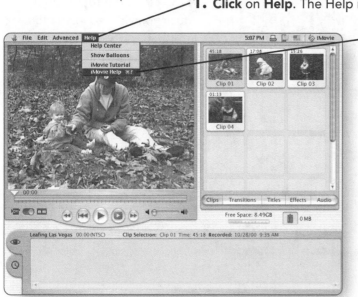

2. **Click** on **iMovie Help**. The iMovie Help window will appear.

3a. **Type** a **topic** in the text box and **click** on **Search**.

OR

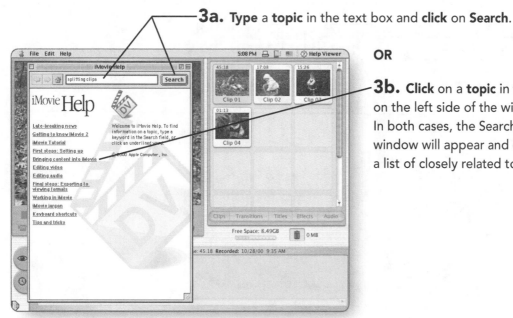

3b. **Click** on a **topic** in the list on the left side of the window. In both cases, the Search Results window will appear and display a list of closely related topics.

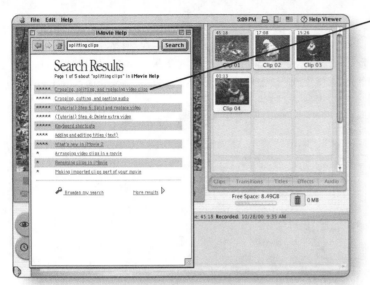

4. **Click** on the **topic** about which you want to learn more. Information about that specific topic will appear in a new window.

5. **Click** on the **close box** to exit Help. The Help window will close.

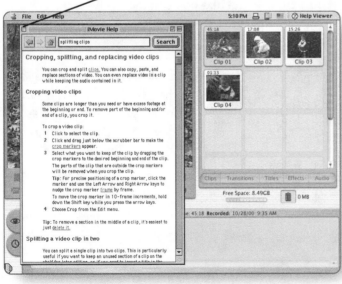

Getting Help from the Help Center

The Help Center allows you to get quick answers to all of your Macintosh questions.

1. **Click** on **Help**. The Help menu will appear.

2. **Click** on **Help Center**. The Help Center window will appear.

3a. **Type** a **topic** in the text box and **click** on **Search**.

OR

3b. **Click** on a **topic** from the available list. A list of subtopics will appear.

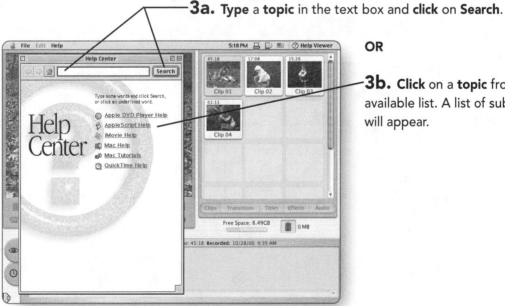

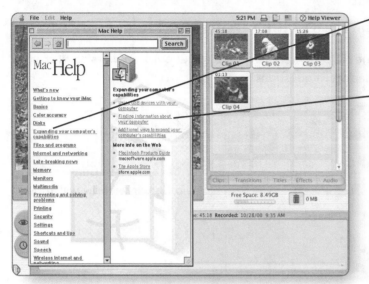

4. Click on a **subtopic**. More specific topics will appear in a list on the right.

5. Click on the **topic** that best fits your question. Detailed answers to your question will appear in the window.

6. Click on the **close box**. The Help window will close.

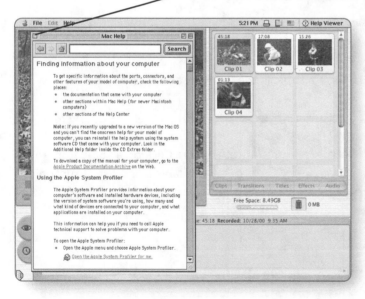

Getting Help from the Balloons

Macintosh computers have a help feature called *balloons* that you can access. With this feature, you can hover your mouse pointer over an icon, button, or tool, and a balloon will appear with an explanation about that particular feature.

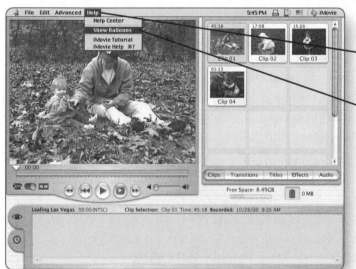

1. Click on **Help**. The Help menu will appear.

2. Click on **Show Balloons**. The option will be selected.

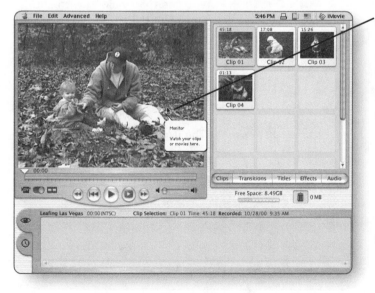

3. Place the **mouse pointer** over an area on the screen about which you want more information. A balloon with a brief description of the screen element will appear.

4. **Click** on **Help**. The Help menu will appear.

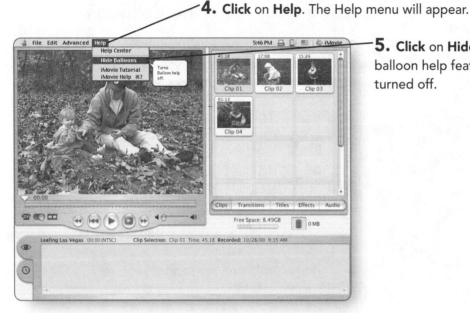

5. **Click** on **Hide Balloons**. The balloon help feature will be turned off.

Running the Help Tutorial

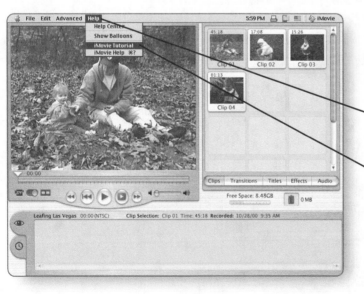

iMovie 2 includes a built-in tutorial with sample clips that you can follow along with and learn from, if you desire.

1. **Click** on **Help**. The Help menu will appear.

2. **Click** on **iMovie Tutorial**. The iMovie Help window will appear.

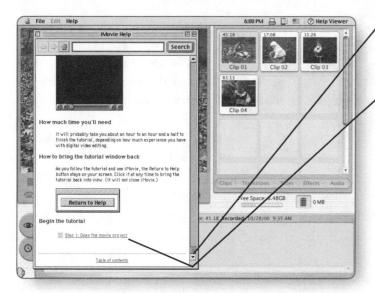

3. Click on the **down arrow** to scroll down to the bottom of the window.

4. Click on **Step 1: Open the movie project**. A description of Step 1 of the tutorial will appear in the window.

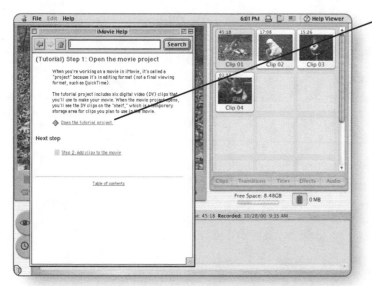

5. Click on **Open the tutorial project**. The tutorial's clips will appear in the Scrolling Shelf.

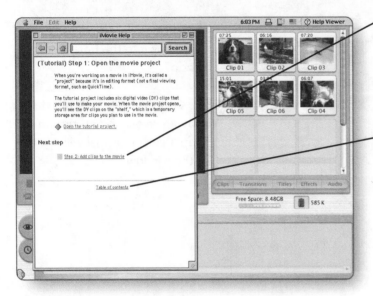

6. Continue to **click** on the succeeding steps in the tutorial and **follow** the **on-screen instructions** to view all of the topics of the tutorial.

7. Optionally, you can **click** on **Table of contents.** A list of specific tutorial topics will appear.

8. Click on a **specific topic.** You will be taken directly to that topic in the tutorial.

9. Click on the **close box**. The Help window will close.

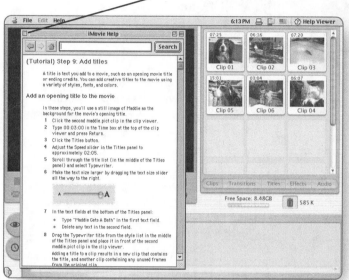

10. Click on **File**. The File menu will appear.

11. Click on **Quit**. A Confirm Save message box will open, asking you if you want to save the changes you made to the tutorial (if you indeed made any changes).

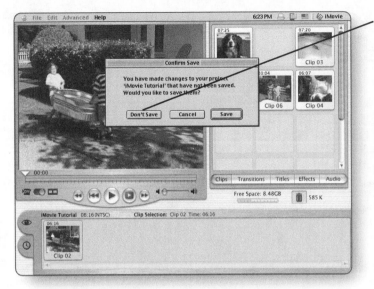

12. Click on **Don't Save**. The tutorial will close.

NOTE

If, for some reason, you want to keep the edited version of the tutorial that you played around with, go ahead and click on Save. Then, whenever you want to go back to the tutorial and open the tutorial project files, you will see the version of the tutorial with the edits you made.

4

Importing Footage

Before you jump in and start editing scenes in your movie, you should have a storyboard picture of your epic in your mind, so that you know what footage you need to gather and import into iMovie. iMovie will help you make the production, but it cannot provide the vision. After you have planned all your shots and captured the footage, you're ready to begin importing and editing the footage. In this chapter, you'll learn how to:

- Switch modes
- Import a clip from your camcorder
- Store clips
- Use the scene-detection feature
- Adjust the quality of video playback
- Import analog video
- Save and open iMovie projects

Switching Modes

iMovie includes two different work modes: Edit and Camera. Before you can begin editing your clips in iMovie, you need to get into Edit mode. If importing digital video clips is on your agenda, you need to jump into Camera mode.

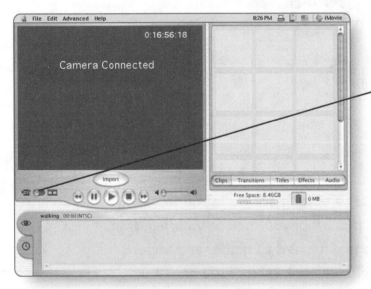

1. If you haven't already done so, **launch iMovie**. iMovie will open.

2. Press and hold the **mouse button** down on the blue toggle switch in the lower-left corner of the Monitor window.

3. Slide the **switch** toward one of the following modes:

- **Camera (the DV icon)**. The blue screen in the Monitor window will display a message indicating whether the camera is connected.

- **Edit (the filmstrip icon)**. The blue screen in the Monitor window will turn to black.

4. Release the **mouse button**. The mode will be selected.

Importing a Clip from Your Digital Video Camera

Once you've captured your award-winning footage, the first thing you need to do is get it into iMovie so that you can begin playing with this exciting editing tool. Make sure your digital video camera is connected to your Mac, your digital videotape of footage is inserted in your camcorder, and the camcorder is on and switched to the VTR setting.

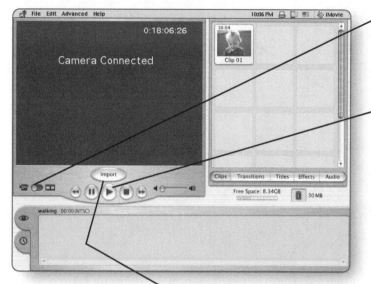

1. Switch to **Camera mode** as you learned to do in the previous section. You will now be able to import your video.

2a. Click on the **Play button** on the Monitor window.

OR

2b. Press the **Play button** on your camcorder. Your video will play in the Monitor window.

3. Click on **Import** in the Monitor window when you are at a scene in your videotape that you want to import into iMovie. The clip will appear in the Scrolling Shelf, with a running time count in the upper-left corner of the clip and the clip number labeled at the bottom of the clip.

NOTE

You can skip steps 2a or 2b if you want to—clicking on Import will immediately import the video from your camcorder. However, if you want more control over what footage you import into iMovie, you might want to press the Play button first and then click on Import when you see the specific footage you want to import.

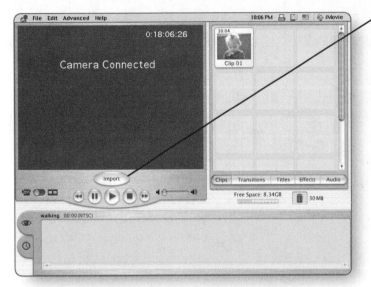

4. Click on **Import** again when you want to stop importing that particular clip. The final time length of the clip will appear in the upper-left corner of the clip.

TIP

Don't worry about importing and ending your clip exactly where you want it. You'll edit the individual clips precisely with cropping tools later. With that in mind, it's best to give yourself some breathing room. Start importing your video a few frames ahead of where you want the final clip to start. Then, stop importing a few frames after where you want the final clip to end. This will ensure that you have all the footage you want in that particular clip, and you can always edit it again later.

Setting the Destination of Your Imported Clips

As you just learned, when you import digital video into iMovie, the clips that you import are automatically saved to the Scrolling Shelf. This is the easiest way to manage your clips in the initial stages of your editing. If you want, however, you can change this setting to automatically save your clips directly into the Clip Viewer.

1. Click on **Edit**. The Edit menu will appear.

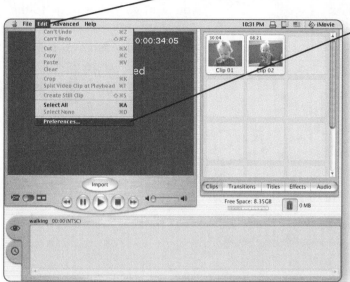

2. Click on **Preferences**. The Preferences dialog box will open.

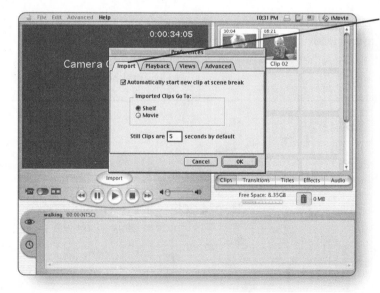

3. Click on the **Import tab**. The tab will move to the front. The Shelf option should already be selected. This means that when you import your video, the clips will go directly into the Scrolling Shelf.

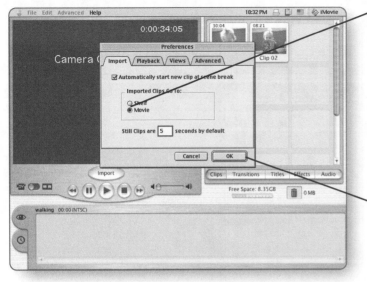

4. Click on the **Movie option** if you want your clips to go to the Clip Viewer. By selecting this option, your video clips will import directly into the Clip Viewer, which you'll learn more about in Chapter 5, "The Cutting Room Floor: Precise and Polished Editing."

5. Click on **OK** to save your changes.

Using iMovie's Scene-Detection Feature

You can import clips using an automatic scene-detection feature. iMovie will automatically find the beginning and end of a scene that you captured and will save it as a clip. If you are a moviemaker who likes to stop and start scenes often, this is a great feature.

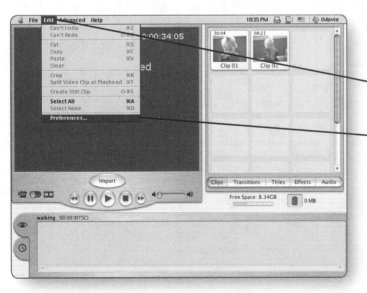

1. Click on **Edit**. The Edit menu will appear.

2. Click on **Preferences**. The Preferences dialog box will open.

3. Click on the **Import tab**, if it isn't already selected. The tab will move to the front.

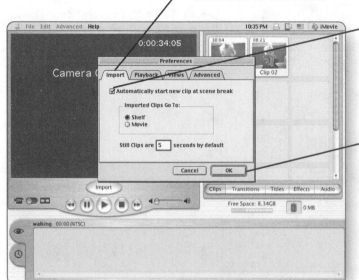

4. Click on the **Automatically start new clip at scene break check box** to insert a check mark. The option will be selected.

5. Click on **OK**. Now, when iMovie detects where you started a scene, a new clip will appear in the Scrolling Shelf (or the Clip Viewer, if you have designated the clips to be imported there). When iMovie detects the end of the scene, that clip will stop importing and a new clip will appear with the next scene you captured. You can just sit back and watch iMovie create the clips for you.

Adjusting the Quality of Video Playback

Depending on how you like to see your video played back on your computer, you can make adjustments accordingly. You have two choices: Smoother Motion and Better Image. Smoother Motion basically gives you smoother video playback, but with a reduced image quality. Better Image gives you crisper image quality but choppier video playback.

1. Click on **Edit**. The Edit menu will appear.

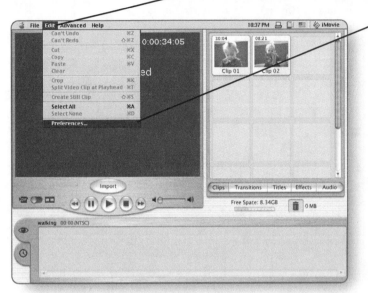

2. Click on **Preferences**. The Preferences dialog box will open.

3. Click on the **Playback tab**, if it isn't already selected. The Playback tab will move to the front.

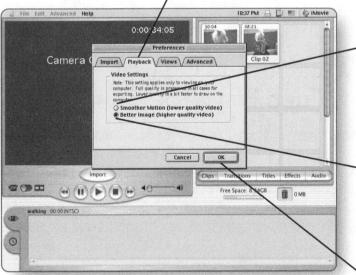

4. Click on **one** of the following:

- **Smoother Motion (lower quality video)**. The Smoother Motion option will decrease visual quality to give you more frames per second during playback.

- **Better Image (higher quality video)**. The Better Image option will give you crisper images, but you will see a choppier playback.

5. Click on **OK**. Your option will take effect.

> **NOTE**
>
> This feature is only for the video playback on your computer screen. These settings do not affect the quality of the movie you make when you export your finished product to videotape or QuickTime, which you will learn how to do in Chapter 10, "Compressing and Exporting Your Movies."

Importing Analog Video

As I mentioned in Chapter 1, "Tools of the Trade," if you don't have a DV camcorder and you want to import analog video, you need a special converter box that will convert the analog video to a digital video signal.

If you have a digital video camera and want to add, say, some old VHS tape footage into iMovie, you can dub the VHS footage onto a DV tape and then import it into iMovie. All you need is a VCR, some A/V connecting cables, a DV camcorder and blank DV tape, and, of course, your VHS footage.

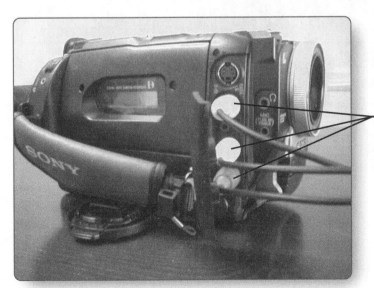

1. **Insert** your **VHS footage** into your VCR, and **insert** a **blank DV tape** into your camcorder.

2. **Attach** one **end** of the A/V connecting cables to the appropriate ports on your camcorder.

3. Attach the other **end** of the A/V connecting cables to the Output ports on your VCR.

4. Confirm that your **camcorder** is set to VTR, and **press** the **Play button** on your VCR. The VHS footage will play in your camcorder . . .

. . . and on your television.

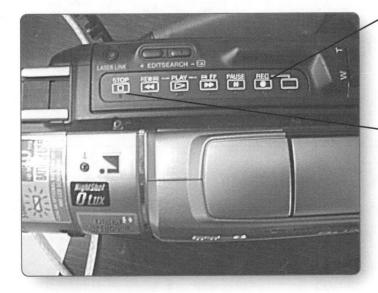

5. Press the **Record button** on your camcorder at the instant you want your footage to start recording onto your DV tape. The footage will start recording.

6. Press the **Stop button** on your camcorder when you want to cease recording the footage. The recording will stop.

You now have your analog video footage on your DV tape, ready to import into iMovie. Just follow the steps in the "Importing a Clip from Your Digital Video Camera" section earlier in this chapter to help you import the clip into iMovie, and you're all done.

NOTE

You'll notice that the footage might be a bit grainy. It's definitely not going to have the sharp quality of your digital videos, but the picture still looks pretty good, and the important thing is that you got it into iMovie.

Saving Your iMovie Project

Now that you've created a new project, imported some footage, and named your project, you need to know how to save this project so you can keep it and make further enhancements at a later date.

1. **Click** on **File**. The File menu will appear.

2. **Click** on **Save Project**. Your project and all of the changes you made to it will be saved.

Opening an Existing iMovie Project

Now that you've learned how to save your project, you need to learn how to open a project and do some more work on it, since you probably haven't made many enhancements just yet. By now you might have imported hours of footage and saved the footage as three or four individual iMovie projects. You can open an existing iMovie project using the Open command.

1. Open iMovie, if it isn't already open. iMovie will open with the last project you worked on in the Scrolling Shelf.

2. Click on **File**. The File menu will appear.

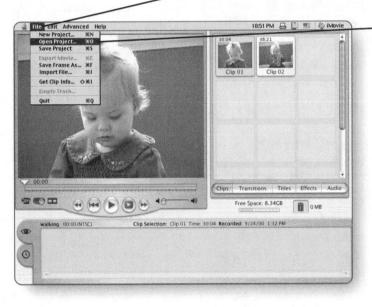

3. Click on **Open Project**. The Open Existing Project dialog box will open.

4. Click on the **pop-up menu**. The pop-up menu will appear.

5. Click on the **folder** (or HD or Desktop) in which your movie resides. A list of your movies will appear.

6. Click on the **movie** that you want to open. The movie will be selected.

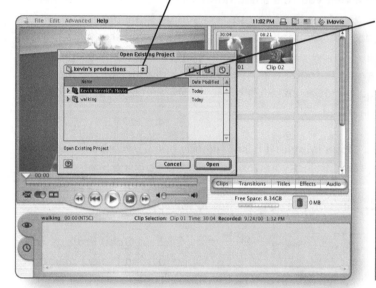

> ### NOTE
> The movie icon you see in Step 6 is actually a folder of your movie project. It houses two icons: the actual iMovie and a Media folder that contains all of the individual clips within the iMovie.

7. Click on **Open**. Another dialog box will open, containing the actual iMovie and the Media folder.

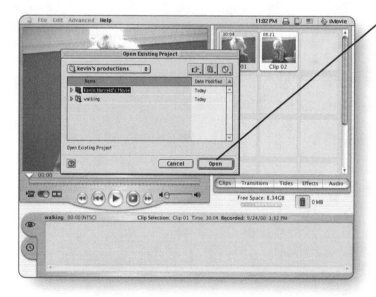

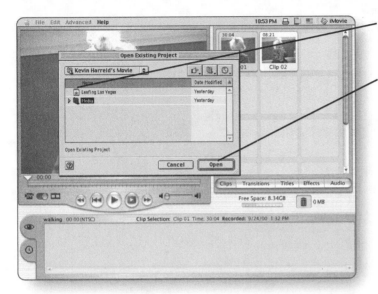

8. Click on the **iMovie icon**. The movie will be selected.

9. Click on **Open**.

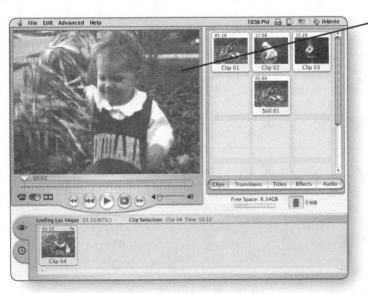

The movie will open.

5

The Cutting Room Floor: Precise and Polished Editing

With iMovie, you can edit your clips to filter out hours of the repetitive footage you take while waiting for your seven-month-old daughter to say "Da-Da." You can make it look as if she said it on cue, even if it did take an entire cassette of videotape. You will learn to appreciate what Hollywood film editors do to make a great film. And the next time you watch the Academy Awards, maybe you won't go to the kitchen to make a sandwich when the Oscar for Best Film Editing is announced. In this chapter, you'll learn how to:

- Select and rename clips
- Crop and split clips
- Restore clips
- Copy and move clips
- Throw clips in the trash

Selecting Clips

You can edit your clips one at a time or work on several at once. It's just a matter of selecting one clip or a group of clips and then starting your work.

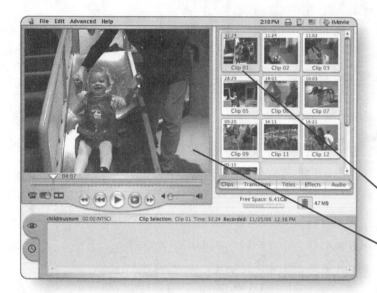

Selecting a Single Clip to Edit

Before you start editing your clips, you have to identify the clip with which you want to work. Selecting a single clip is a simple task.

1. In the Scrolling Shelf, **click** on the **clip** you want to edit.

The clip will be highlighted and will appear in the Monitor window.

NOTE

You might notice that a long blue bar appears under the Monitor window after you select your clip. This is called the Scrubber bar. You will learn more about this editing tool in later sections of this chapter, starting with the "Cropping Clips" section.

Selecting Multiple Clips

There might be times when you need to select more than one clip at a time (such as when you are moving clips from the Scrolling Shelf to the Clip Viewer or to the trash, both of which you'll learn about later in this chapter).

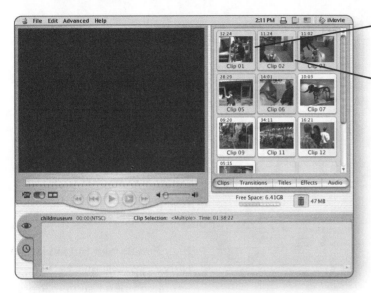

1. Click on a **clip**. The clip will be selected.

2. Press and hold the **Shift key** and continue to **click** on any other **clips** that you want to select. All the clips that you click on will be highlighted in yellow, indicating that they are selected, and the Monitor window will show a black screen.

3. Click anywhere outside the Scrolling Shelf if you wish to deselect the group of clips. The highlighted clips will be deselected.

Playing Clips

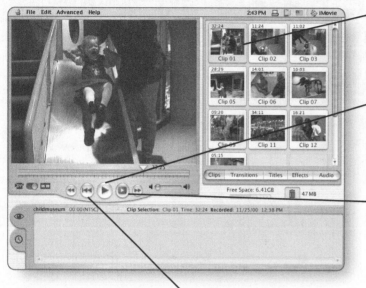

1. **Click** on a **clip or clips**, as described in the previous section. The clip or clips will be selected.

2. **Click** on the **Play button**. The clip or clips will play.

3. **Click** on any of the other **buttons**:

- **Play Full-Screen button**. The clip or clips will play on your entire computer screen. Press the Esc key to return to the iMovie screen.

- **Home button**. You will be returned to the beginning of the clip or clips.

- **Rewind button**. Your clip(s) will rewind. Click on this button again to stop rewinding.

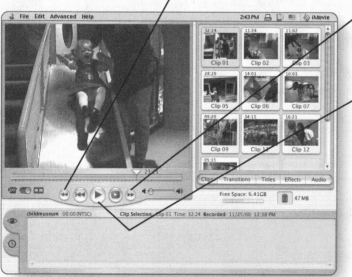

- **Fast-Forward button**. Your clip(s) will fast-forward. Click on this button again to stop fast-forwarding.

- **Play button**. Your clip will stop playing if you click on this button again during playback.

Renaming a Clip

In iMovie 2, you can access a clip's name, find out its size, and change how its audio fades in or fades out. You can even change the name of the clip.

1. Double-click on a **clip**. The clip's Clip Info box will open. The following information is included in this box:

- **Name**. This is the temporary name of the clip that iMovie assigns. Renaming a clip will help you remember what that clip contains.

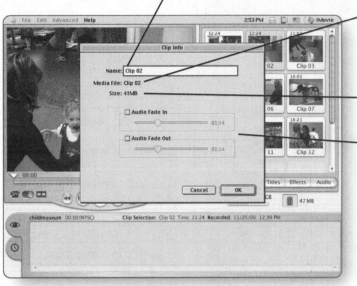

- **Media File**. This is the permanent file name of the clip that iMovie remembers. This name can't be changed.

- **Size**. This shows you the size of the clip.

- **Audio Fade In/Out**. This feature allows you to fade the audio of the clip in and out. You'll learn more about this in Chapter 8, "Audio: Adding Soundtracks, Scores, Sounds, and Narration."

2. Select the **text** in the Name text box to rename the clip. The text will be highlighted.

3. Type the **new name** of your clip.

4. Click on **OK**. The new name will take effect.

NOTE

Notice that when you double-click on the clip that you just renamed, your clip shows the new name in the Name text box, but also displays the original clip name that iMovie gave it in the Media File section. This is because iMovie doesn't rename the media clips housed in the Media folder within an iMovie project. You'll learn more about media clips in Chapter 10, "Compressing and Exporting Your Movies."

Cropping Clips

Remember when I said you'd have a chance to crop out the unwanted footage from the beginning or end of your clips? Here's your chance.

1. Click on the **clip** you want to crop. The clip will appear in the Monitor window.

2. Click and hold the **mouse button** on the playhead (the downward-facing triangle on top of the Scrubber bar) and **drag** the **playhead** to approximately where you want to crop out the beginning of your footage (that is, to where you want the remaining footage to start).

3. Release the **mouse button**. The playhead will be in position.

NOTE

Notice that as you drag the playhead, a number (timecode) appears to the right of it. That number indicates the exact time location in your clip. For example, 1:29 means that you are 1 second and 29 frames into the clip.

4. Press the **Shift key** and **click** on a **hash mark** (the little lines below the Scrubber bar) approximately where you want to crop out the end of your clip (that is, where you want the remaining footage to end). The middle section of the Scrubber bar will turn yellow, and small triangular markers will appear below it at each end of the yellow section. This section represents the part of the clip that will be saved. The parts before and after this section of the clip will eventually be cropped out.

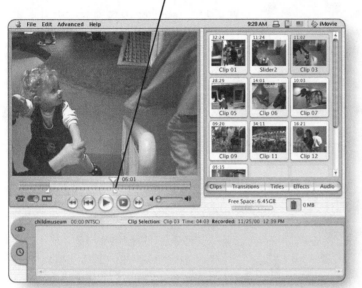

5. Click and hold the **mouse button** on the small triangular crop markers and drag them left or right to precisely where you want to crop out the beginning and end of your clip. The clip will rewind or play forward in the Monitor window as you drag the markers.

6. Release the **mouse button**. The crop markers will be set exactly where you want them.

> ### TIP
> To have even more precise control over where to place your crop markers, use the left and right arrow keys on your keyboard. Just click on one of the crop markers and then tap the left or right arrow keys and watch the footage play frame by frame in the Monitor window.

7. Click on **Edit**. The Edit menu will appear.

8. Click on **Crop**. The footage of your clip before and after the section marked by the yellow bar will be cropped.

Undoing a Crop

Suppose you've cropped a clip and you don't like how it looks. You can use the Undo feature to correct a mistake, but only immediately after you make the erroneous crop. The Undo feature "undoes" the most recent action you've taken.

1. Click on **Edit**. The Edit menu will appear.

2. Click on **Undo Crop**. The clip will go back to its previously saved state.

NOTE

The Undo feature works for any action that you've just taken and want to reverse, not just cropping. Follow the previous steps to undo anything. Just remember, you can only undo the most recent action. Also, you cannot use Undo after performing a Save or Save As, so be certain about the changes you are making to your clip before you save. Follow the steps in the next section, "Restoring Clips," if you need to restore a clip to its original state after saving changes.

Restoring Clips

If you've made several edits to a clip, but you now want to revert to the clip's original state, you can use iMovie's Restore Clip feature.

1. **Click** on the **clip** that you want to restore. The clip will be selected.

2. Click on **Advanced**. The Advanced menu will appear.

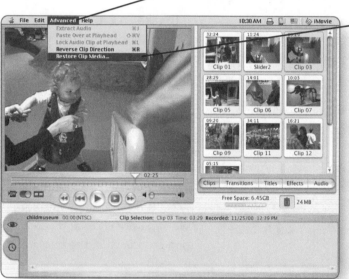

3. Click on **Restore Clip Media**. A Confirm message box will appear, asking you whether you want to restore the clip's original attributes.

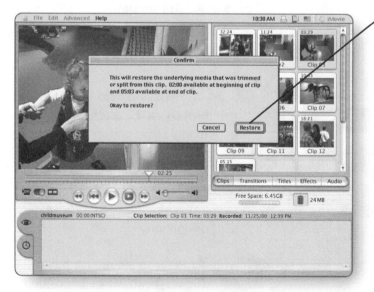

4. Click on **Restore**. The clip will be restored.

NOTE

You can only restore a clip to its original state if you have not already emptied the trash. Once you have emptied the trash containing the edited footage from the clip you want to restore, iMovie has no way to retrieve the media files that you have permanently deleted.

Splitting Clips

The split-clip feature allows you to take an imported clip and split it into two separate clips. This is important when you have imported a clip of a certain scene and you want the clip to have a transition (which you'll learn about in Chapter 6, "Adding Stylish Transitions"), or you want parts of the scene to be in different places in your finished movie. Also, you might have footage in the middle of a clip that you want to crop out. By splitting the clip, you create two separate clips, and you can then crop each at the beginning and end.

1. Click on the **clip** you want to split. The clip will appear in the Monitor window.

2. Press and hold the **mouse button** on the playhead (the triangle icon on top of the Scrubber bar) and drag it to the spot where you want to split the clip. Remember, you can use the arrow keys for more precise navigation.

3. Release the **mouse button**. The playhead will be in position.

4. **Click** on **Edit**. The Edit menu will appear.

5. **Click** on **Split Video Clip at Playhead**. The single clip will become two separate clips, and they both will appear in the Scrolling Shelf.

Notice that the first part of the clip retains the original name of the clip, whereas the second part of the clip gets a /1 attached to the clip name.

Copying Clips

Instead of splitting a clip in two, maybe you want an exact copy of a clip. One reason for copying a clip is to leave one version of the clip in its original form while testing effects and edits on the other version. By making a copy, you will always have the original footage exactly the way you captured it.

1. Click on the **clip** you want to copy. The clip will be selected.

2. Click on **Edit**. The Edit menu will appear.

3. Click on **Copy**. A copy of the clip will be made and placed on a clipboard.

4. Click on **Edit**. The Edit menu will appear.

5. Click on **Paste**. The copied clip will appear on the Scrolling Shelf.

Notice that the copied clip has the same name as the original. You can always change the name by using the method you learned earlier in this chapter.

Moving Clips from the Scrolling Shelf to the Clip Viewer

After cropping a clip just the way you like it, you might want to put it on the Clip Viewer. The Clip Viewer is the video clip section of the Timeline, where you can see your movie come together chronologically. You can put as many clips as you want, in any order you want, on the Clip Viewer. The Timeline houses the Clip Viewer and the Timeline Viewer, and is where you'll shuffle clips around, add transitions between clips, add audio effects, and so on. You'll learn all about the special features of the Timeline as you read the rest of the chapters in this book. For now, you need to get the clips to the Clip Viewer.

1. Click on the **Clip Viewer tab** of the Timeline, if it isn't already selected. The Clip Viewer tab will move to the front.

2. Click and hold the **mouse button** on the clip in the Scrolling Shelf that you want to move to the Clip Viewer and **drag** the **clip** down to the Clip Viewer.

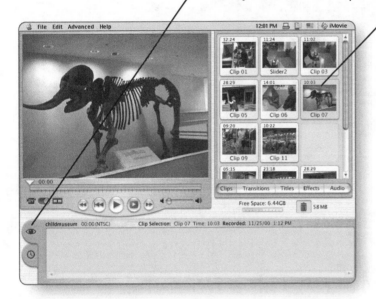

3. Release the **mouse button**. The clip will appear in the Clip Viewer.

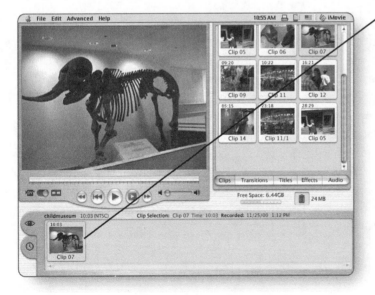

4. Click and hold the **mouse button** on another clip in the Scrolling Shelf that you want to move to the Clip Viewer.

5. Drag the **clip**, while still holding down the mouse button, before or after the clip that's already in the Clip Viewer, depending on where in the final movie you want this clip to appear. A box will highlight where the clip will be placed in the Clip Viewer.

6. Release the **mouse button**. The clip will appear in the Clip Viewer.

NOTE

Often, you will want to insert a new clip in between multiple clips in the Clip Viewer. Just drag the new clip to the desired spot in the Clip Viewer. When the small space appears between the two clips to make room for the new clip, release the mouse button. Your clip will be inserted between the two clips already in the Clip Viewer.

Trashing Clips

Do you have clips that you've decided not to use? Dump them in the trash can. Just remember, once you empty the trash, you can't retrieve anything that was in it.

1. Press and hold the **mouse button** on the clip you want to delete and **drag** the **clip** to the trash can icon at the bottom of the Shelf.

2. Release the **mouse button** when the trash can is highlighted. The clip will be thrown away.

3. Click on **File**. The File menu will appear.

4. Click on **Empty Trash**. The Confirm message box will open.

5. Click on **OK**. The trash will be emptied.

Part II Review Questions

1. How do you create your first iMovie project? *See Creating a New Project in Chapter 3*

2. How do you view your video on the computer screen? *See Previewing Your Video in the Monitor Window in Chapter 3*

3. How do you get your video into iMovie? *See Importing a Clip from Your Digital Video Camera in Chapter 4*

4. How do you adjust the quality of your video clips in iMovie? *See Adjusting the Quality of Video Playback in Chapter 4*

5. How do you automatically find the beginning and end of a video scene that you captured and save that scene as a clip? *See Using iMovie's Scene-Detection Feature in Chapter 4*

6. How do you give a name to a clip? *See Renaming a Clip in Chapter 5*

7. How do you cut out unwanted footage from individual clips? *See Cropping Clips in Chapter 5*

8. How can you split one clip into two separate clips? *See Splitting Clips in Chapter 5*

9. How can you put a clip in the Clip Viewer? *See Moving Clips from the Scrolling Shelf to the Clip Viewer in Chapter 5*

10. How do you make an exact copy of a clip? *See Copying Clips in Chapter 5*

PART III

iMovie
Effects and
Post-Production

6

Adding Stylish Transitions

Transitions can make your movie look seamless. Instead of straight cuts from one scene to the next, you can apply a number of different transition effects to the breaks in action. The transitions in iMovie add stylish cross-fades, dissolves, washes, and other effects to your videos. In this chapter, you'll learn how to:

- Update your set of transitions
- Select a transition
- Set the speed of a transition
- Add, change, and delete transitions
- Insert a clip in the middle of a transition

Updating Your Set of Transitions

Apple has a plug-in pack of additional transitions, titles, and effects available on its Web site for iMovie 2. Before you get the plug-in pack, you'll need to update iMovie 2 to iMovie version 2.0.1. It is a free update for those who have iMovie 2, and it enables you to use the new features in the plug-in pack.

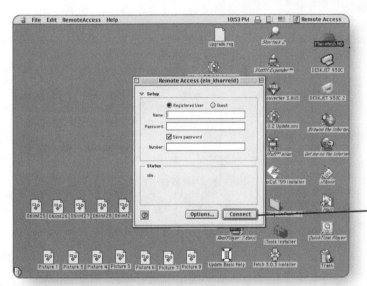

To learn how to update your iMovie 2 software to iMovie 2.0.1, turn to Appendix A, "Acquiring and Installing iMovie 2." After you've had success with that, connect to the Internet and go to Apple's Web site to download the transition, title, and effect plug-ins.

1. Connect to the **Internet**. Your browser window will open.

2. Go to **Apple's iMovie page** (http://www.apple.com/imovie). The page will appear.

NOTE

Your steps for connecting to the Internet will vary, depending on your configuration and what ISP (*Internet Service Provider*) you use.

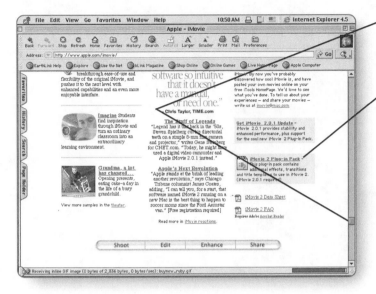

3. **Scroll** down the **page** until you reach the iMovie 2 Plug-in Pack link.

4. **Click** on the **iMovie 2 Plug-in Pack link**. The plug-in pack will download to your desktop.

5. **Exit** your **browser**. Your browser will close.

6. **Exit iMovie**, if you have it running. The program will close.

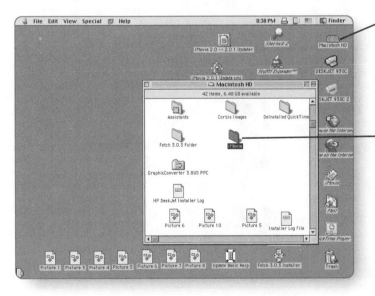

7. **Double-click** on the **Macintosh HD icon** on your desktop. A window showing the contents of your hard drive will appear.

8. **Double-click** on the **iMovie folder**. The iMovie window will appear.

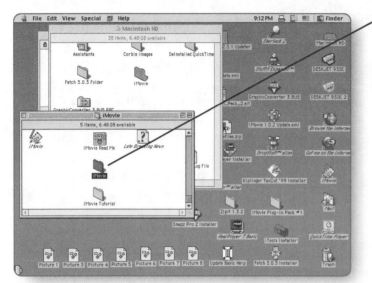

9. Double-click on the **iMovie folder** in the iMovie window. A second iMovie window will appear.

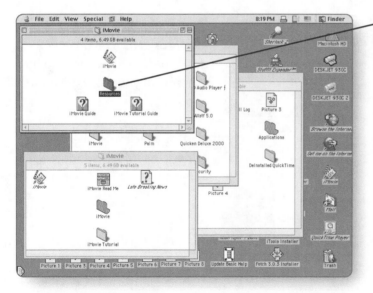

10. Double-click on the **Resources folder**. The Resources window will appear.

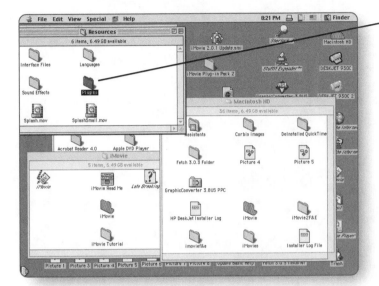

11. Double-click on the **Plugins folder**. The Plugins window will appear.

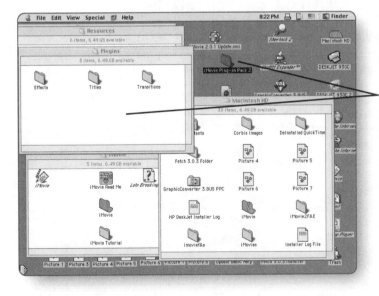

12. Locate the **iMovie Plug-in Pack 2 folder icon** on your desktop.

13. Press and hold the **mouse button** on the iMovie Plug-in Pack 2 folder icon and **drag** the **folder** into the Plugins folder.

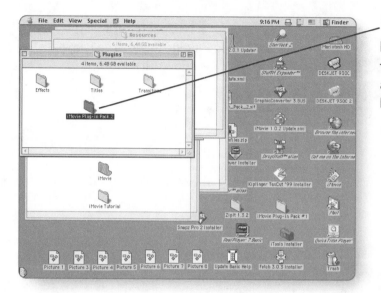

14. Release the **mouse button**. The new transitions, titles, and effects will be available the next time you launch iMovie.

Selecting a Transition

Selecting a transition for your movie takes a bit of forethought. You have the opportunity to play with the different effects to see what works best with your movie. You can mix and match different transitions, but it's usually best to stay simple and consistent and use the same effect throughout. Try some of the effects to see what works best with your footage.

1. Move your **clips** from the Scrolling Shelf to the Clip Viewer, if they're not already there. Try to arrange the clips in the order you want them. (You can rearrange the clips later, but it's best to get them close to how you want them at this time.)

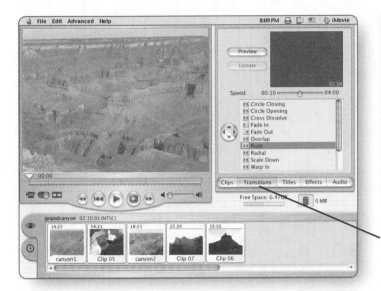

NOTE

Go back to Chapter 5, "The Cutting Room Floor: Precise and Polished Editing," if you need a refresher on how to move your clips from the Scrolling Shelf to the Clip Viewer.

2. **Click** on **Transitions** in the Design panel. The Transitions panel will appear.

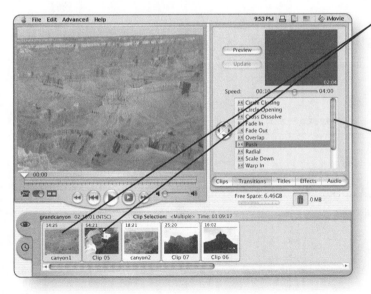

3. **Select** a **clip or series of clips** on which you want to preview the effects of a transition. The clip or clips will be selected.

4. **Drag** the **scroll bar** in the Transitions panel up or down to view the available selections.

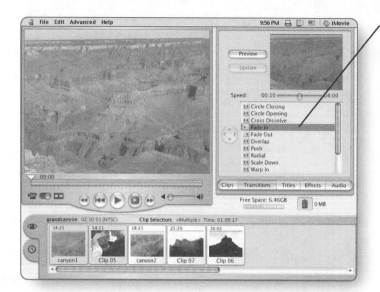

5. Click on a **transition effect**. The effect will quickly appear in the preview window (the small window in the Transitions panel).

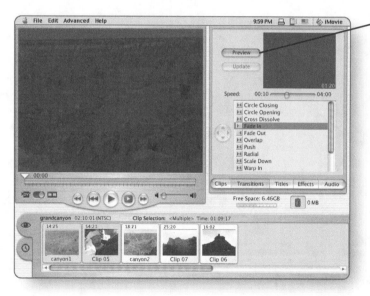

6. Click on **Preview**. The transition effect and how it looks with the clip(s) you selected will appear in the Monitor window. This will give you a better idea of how a transition will look than the small preview window will.

Setting Transition Speed

You will need to assign a duration, or speed, to your transitions. If you want a slow, deliberate transition effect between your clips, you should increase the duration. If you want just a slight hint of a transition effect, reduce the duration.

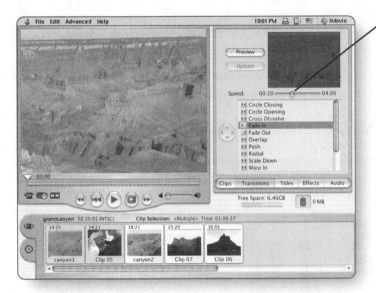

1. **Click and hold** the **mouse button** on the Speed slider in the Transitions panel.

2a. **Drag** the **slider** left to reduce the duration of the transition.

OR

2b. **Drag** the **slider** right to increase the duration of the transition. The transition time will appear in the lower-right corner of the preview window as you drag the slider.

NOTE

The number at the left end of the Speed slider, 00:10, or 10 frames, represents the minimum length that you can set for a transition. The number at the right end of the Speed slider, 04:00, or 4 seconds, represents the maximum length that you can set for a transition. As you drag the slider, the duration appears in the lower-right corner of the preview window. For example, 01:20 means that your transition is 1 second and 20 frames in length.

3. **Release** the **mouse button** when you reach the desired duration. The transition effect you chose, as well as the duration you just established, will be shown in the preview window.

> ### NOTE
>
> The longer the transition, the longer iMovie takes to render the transition. *Rendering* is when iMovie creates video frames for a transition. You might want to keep this in mind when you are determining how large you want your finished movie to be, and how you eventually plan to export your movie. For example, if you are planning to send this movie in an e-mail to your relatives, you might want to keep the transitions short and sweet.

Adding the Transition

Now that you've thought about the effect that you want for your movie, selected a transition, and set the duration, you need to add the transition.

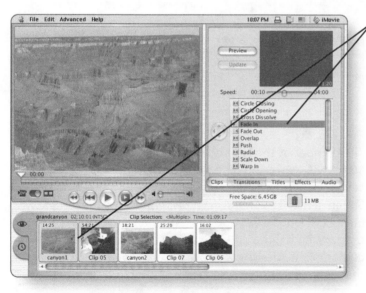

1. **Press and hold** the **mouse button** on the transition you selected and **drag** the **transition** down to where you want to apply the effect. The clips will move over a tad to make room for the transition.

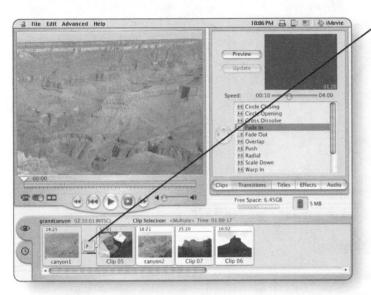

2. Release the **mouse button** and **drop** the **transition**. A monitor icon will appear where you added the transition. A red bar will appear and slowly extend at the bottom of the monitor icon. This is iMovie rendering the transition.

3. Repeat this **process** to add more transitions.

Why Use Certain Transitions?

Most of the transitions in iMovie must be placed between two clips because they utilize both clips in their effect. Cross Dissolve and Push are examples of transitions that need to use two clips to produce their effect.

Certain transition effects work best when you use them in combination or at the beginning or end of your movie. The Fade and Wash transitions are two such effects. For example, adding a Wash Out transition to the end of one clip and then attaching the Wash In transition to the beginning of the following clip creates a smoother effect. A Fade In transition can be placed before the first clip in your movie, and a Fade Out at the end of the last clip.

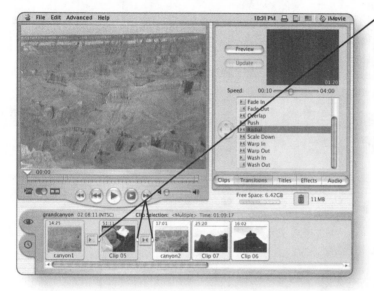

Notice in the Clip Viewer that there are tabs on the transition's monitor icon that attach to the clips associated with the transition. These tabs indicate whether the selected transition effect uses one or both of the clips surrounding it.

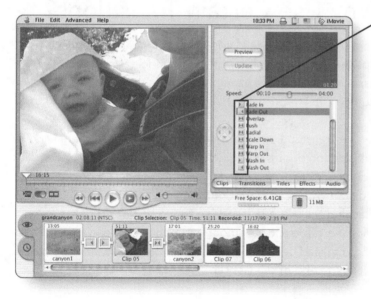

You can also see whether a transition uses one clip or two by looking in the Transitions panel. To the left of each of the transition names are small green boxes. If a transition has a green box with two arrows pointing toward each other, then the transition requires a clip on each side for its effect. If a transition has a green box with only one arrow in it, then it requires only one clip for its effect (the clip in the direction to which the arrow points).

NOTE

The transition duration cannot be longer than the corresponding clip's duration. You will get an error message if you try to attach a transition that is longer than the clip to which you want to attach it.

Another thing to keep in mind is not to overuse transitions. Many times video editors get overzealous and add transitions everywhere. A straight cut between scenes is effective for many productions. The next time you go to the movies, check out how many times special effects for transitions are used between scenes and how many times just a simple cut is used.

Changing a Transition

Change your mind about using that Wash Out transition? You can change the style or duration, or both, of any transition.

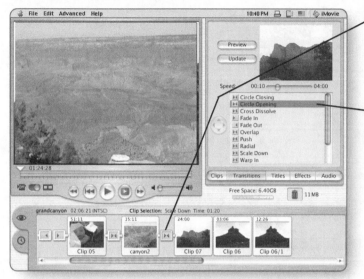

1. Click on the **transition** in the Clip Viewer that you want to change. The transition will be selected.

2. Click on a **new transition style** in the Transitions panel. The new style will be selected.

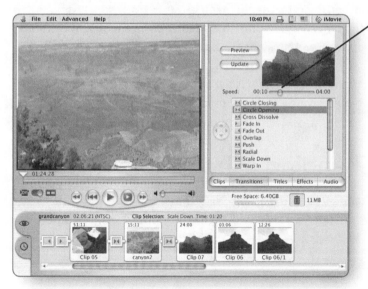

3. Move the **Speed slider** to a new duration. The new duration will be selected.

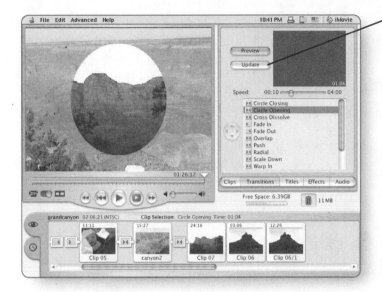

4. **Click** on **Update**. The changes will take effect, and the new transition will be rendered.

Deleting a Transition

Want to get rid of a transition altogether? You can completely delete the transition. The few frames of the two clips that were used with the transition will be restored after you delete the transition.

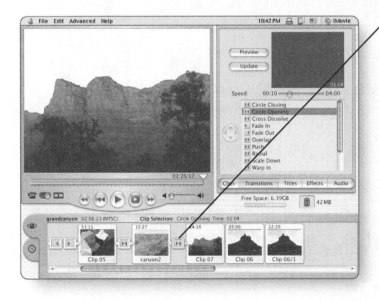

1. **Click** on the **transition** in the Clip Viewer that you want to delete. The transition will be selected.

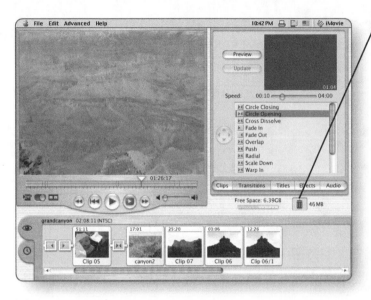

2. **Click and hold** the **mouse button** on the transition you want to delete and **drag** the **transition** to the trash can.

3. **Release** the **mouse button**. The transition will be deleted.

NOTE

You can also delete a transition by clicking on the transition you want to delete and then pressing the Delete key.

Inserting a Clip Where a Transition Exists

Let's say you decide that you want to add a new clip between two existing clips connected by a transition, and you want that same transition to appear on either side of the new clip. If you drag the new clip to the Clip Viewer, iMovie doesn't open a space for you to drop the clip. Sometimes you just have to improvise.

1. **Click** on the **transition** in the Clip Viewer where you want to add your new clip. The transition will be selected.

2. **Press** the **Delete key**. The transition will be deleted.

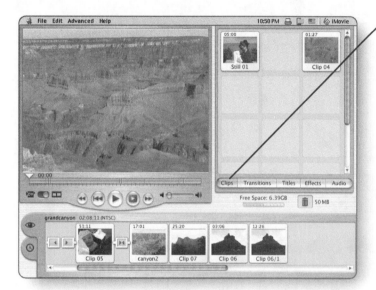

3. Click on **Clips** in the Design panel. The Scrolling Shelf will appear.

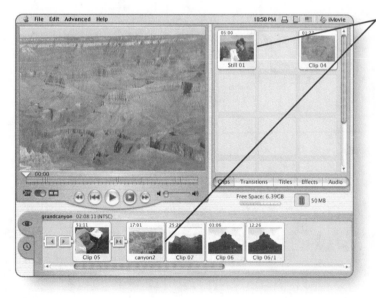

4. Drag the **new clip** from the Scrolling Shelf to the area where you deleted the transition in the Clip Viewer.

5. Release the **mouse button**. The clip will appear in position between the clips.

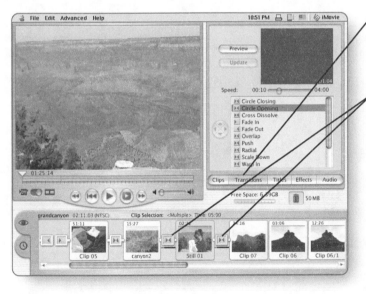

6. Click on **Transitions** in the Design panel. The Transitions panel will appear.

7. Add transitions between the clip you just dragged to the Clip Viewer and the clips on either side of it. In doing so, you have fabricated "splitting" your transition in two and inserting a clip.

7

Text in iMovie: Rolling Titles, Credits, and Captions

A picture is worth a thousand words, but sometimes you just need to spell it out for your audience. Using text in your movies allows you to give titles to your epics, provide explanation, and give credit where credit is due. Titles can add personality, which goes a long way. In this chapter, you'll learn how to:

- Select a title style and background
- Work with font styles and colors
- Adjust the duration of your title
- Position your title
- Change or delete your title

Opening the Titles Panel

The Titles option is located at the bottom of the Design panel, along with the Clips, Transitions, Effects, and Audio options. You open the Titles panel the same way you opened the Transitions panel in Chapter 6, "Adding Stylish Transitions."

1. Move your **clips** from the Scrolling Shelf to the Clip Viewer, if you haven't done so already.

NOTE

You must have your clips in the Clip Viewer to add the title effects to your movie. You can't add titles to clips while they are in the Scrolling Shelf.

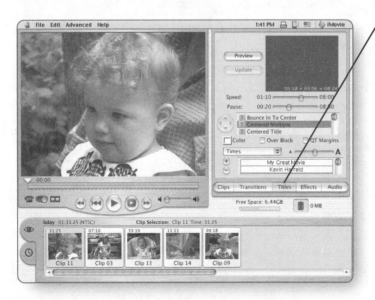

2. Click on **Titles** in the Design panel. The Titles panel will appear.

3. Click on **Clips** or any of the other Design panel options to "close" the Titles panel. The Titles panel will disappear.

NOTE

After learning about iMovie 2's title effects in this chapter, check out Chapter 12, "Tricks with Text," to learn what else you can do with text in iMovie.

Selecting a Title Style

Just below the preview window and the Speed and Pause slider bars in the Titles panel is a list of the title styles available for you to use.

1. Click on a **clip** on which you want to place a title. The clip will be selected.

2. Drag the **scroll bar** in the title styles window to search through the different styles available.

3. Click on a **style name**. The title style will quickly preview in the small preview window.

4. Click on **Preview**. The title style will preview in the Monitor window. This will give you a better look at the style.

Typing Your Title Text

Depending on the style of title you choose, different title text boxes will be available. Some styles allow you to type in long blocks of text or scrolling credits. Others allow you to simply add a short, one-line billboard. You'll see what's available after you select a style.

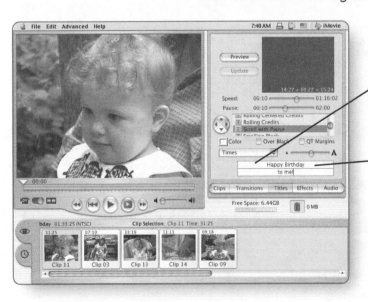

1. Click in the **title text box**. The default text will be highlighted.

2. Type the **title** you want for your movie.

3. Click on **Preview**. Your title will preview in the Monitor window.

Selecting a Title Background

There are three ways you can show the opening title for your movie: over a video clip, over a plain black screen, or over a still image. The first two options can be chosen directly from the Titles panel and are described in the following steps. See Chapter 11, "iMovie 2 and Still Images," for more information about the third option.

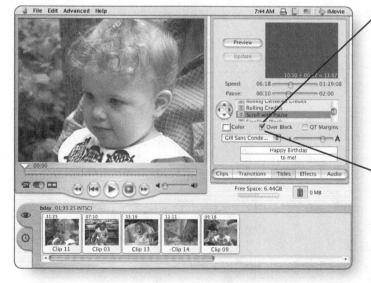

1a. Click on the **check box** to the left of Over Black to insert a check mark. This will allow your title to be shown over a black background rather than over a video clip.

OR

1b. Leave the **check box** to the left of Over Black unchecked and **click** on the **clip** to which you want to add your title. This will allow you to use the video clip as the background for your title.

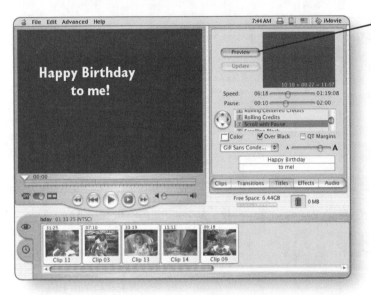

2. Click on **Preview**. The title on the video clip or black background will appear in the Monitor window.

Selecting Apple's Still Files as Backgrounds

You're not limited to using a black page or a video clip as the background for your title. You can take any still image file (providing it is in JPEG, PICT, GIF, BMP, or Photoshop format), insert it into your movie, and then add the title to that image. You'll learn how to do this in Chapter 11, "iMovie 2 and Still Images." Apple has a library of appropriate stills for use as backgrounds for your titles or credits.

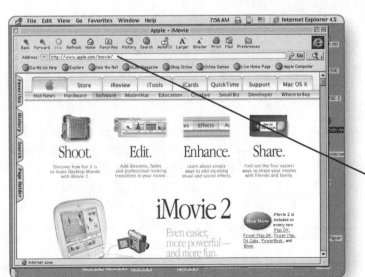

1. Go to **Apple's iMovie page** (http://www.apple.com/imovie).

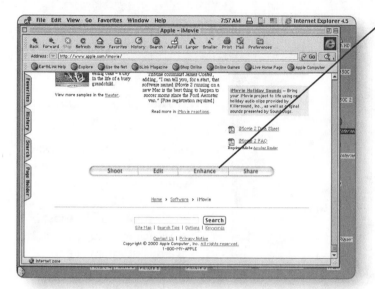

2. Scroll down to the bottom of the page and **click** on **Enhance**. The Enhance page will appear.

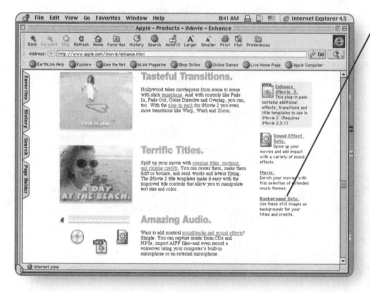

3. Scroll down the page and **click** on the **Background Sets link**. The Background Sets page will appear.

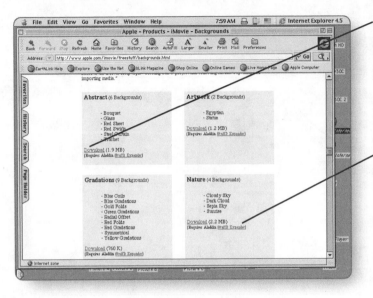

4. **Click** on the **Download link** for a background set that appeals to you. The set will download to your desktop.

NOTE

Some of these background sets require you to have the StuffIt Expander program on your machine to open the downloaded file. Most new Macintosh computers have this program already installed. If for some reason you do not have it, however, you should either download a background set that does not require StuffIt Expander, or download StuffIt Expander by following the StuffIt Expander link. The software is free. Each of the background sets will tell you whether or not you need it.

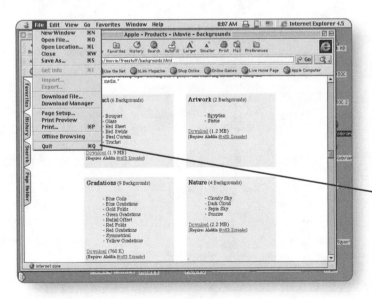

5. **Exit** your **browser**. Your browser will close.

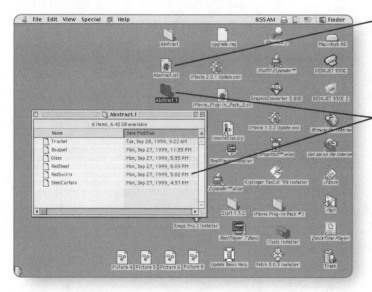

6. Double-click on the **desktop icon** of the Background Set that you downloaded. The folder will extract to your desktop.

7. Open the **folder** and **double-click** on a background **image**. The image will appear.

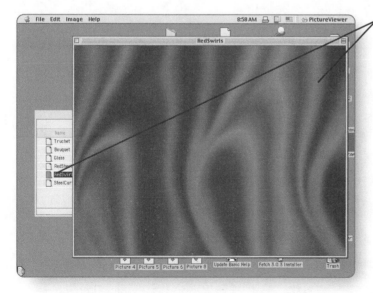

Now you have a cool image to use as a backdrop for a title. Check out Chapter 11, "iMovie 2 and Still Images," to learn how to insert the image in iMovie 2.

Working with Fonts

Choosing a font for your movie title sets the tone for your whole epic. Different font styles, sizes, and colors say various things to the audience. Also, you want your fonts to be easily viewable by your audience.

Selecting a Font Style

It's important to choose the correct font for your movie, since different fonts will set different tones for your movie. For example, a thicker, bolder font makes a strong impression, whereas a smaller, more delicate font sets a more gentle mood.

1. Select the **clip** on which you want your title to appear or **click** on the **Over Black check box** to select a black background for your title.

2. Click on the **font styles pop-up menu**. A list of fonts will appear.

> **NOTE**
>
> Another thing to keep in mind when selecting a font style is how your movie will be shown to your audience. Although a thin, script-type font might look nice on your computer monitor, it probably won't look very good in a QuickTime movie. It's usually best to use bolder, simpler fonts. The key is to make sure that any text in your movie will be readable in any format.

3. **Click** on a **font** from the list. The font will preview in the preview window.

4. **Click** on **Preview**. Your selection will appear in the Monitor window.

Selecting a Font Color

Selecting a font color is also something to consider. You need to select a color that will show up well when it is superimposed on your video or background.

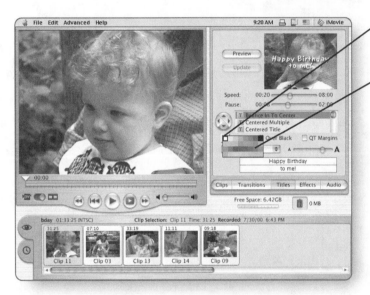

1. Click on the **Color box**. A color palette will appear.

2. Double-click on a **color**.

The color will be selected and will preview in the small preview window.

3. Click on **Preview**. Your selection will appear in the Monitor window.

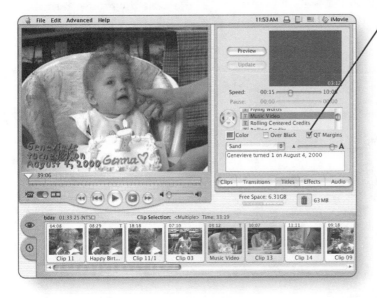

NOTE

iMovie 2's titles are safe for rebroadcast on your TV screen. That is, there is no threat of a title being too close to the edges of the TV screen and getting chopped off. But what if you don't plan to show your movie on TV, and you want to have the title extend to the edges of the frame? For example, there is no danger of losing titles close to the edges of the frames in QuickTime movies. If you plan to show your movie as a QuickTime production (see Chapter 10, "Compressing and Exporting Your Movies" for more information on QuickTime), you should check the QT Margins box.

Selecting a Font Size

It is also important to select an appropriate font size for your text. Again, you want to ensure that people can read the text you put in your iMovie.

1. Press and hold your **mouse button** on the font size slider and **drag** the **slider** left to reduce the font size or right to enlarge it. Your title will get larger or smaller in the preview window as you drag the slider.

2. Release the **mouse button**. Your font size will be set.

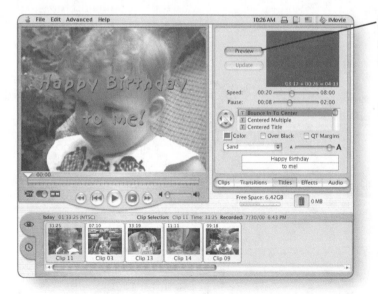

3. Click on **Preview**. Your selection will appear in the Monitor window.

Adjusting the Duration and Pause of Your Title

With most of the title styles, you need to adjust your title's duration and the pause following it. Two slider bars in the Titles panel allow you to set the speed at which your title effect does its trick, and the length of the pause once your title style finishes its effect. Unless you want your title or credits to roll over more than one video clip, your title duration must be less than the duration of the clip on which you want the title to appear.

1. **Press and hold** the **mouse button** on the Speed slider bar and **drag** the **slider bar** left to decrease the duration or right to increase the duration. The title's duration will change accordingly.

2. **Release** the **mouse button**. Your duration will be set.

NOTE

The minimum and maximum durations of the title styles in iMovie are not all the same. As you click on title names in the title styles window, you'll notice that the numbers on the left and right ends of the slider bar change.

3. Press and hold the **mouse button** on the Pause slider bar and **drag** the **slider bar** left to decrease the length of the pause or right to increase the length of the pause.

4. Release the **mouse button**. Your pause will be set.

NOTE

Notice in the lower-right corner of the small preview window that the times chosen by moving the Speed and Pause sliders are added together to give you a grand total for your title's duration. Remember that the first number represents seconds and the second number represents frames. For example, 01:29 means that the total duration of your title is 1 second, 29 frames.

Positioning Your Title

There will be times when you want to position your title at a certain place and a certain point of time in your clip. However, certain title styles won't allow you to align text exactly where you want it. If you need to align your title in an area other than in the center of a clip, make sure you choose a title style that allows you to do this. You will know if you can alter the alignment or scrolling direction of a certain title if the alignment and scrolling dial becomes active when you select the title style.

Specifying Alignment and Scrolling Direction

With some title styles, you can specify the alignment or scrolling direction of the titles.

1. **Click** on a **title style** in the style box. If the dial to the left of the title styles window becomes active, you can adjust the alignment or scrolling direction of that particular style. If the dial remains grayed out, you're out of luck.

2. **Click** on the **up, down, left, or right arrow** of the dial. The alignment or scrolling direction of your selection will be adjusted accordingly.

Setting the Exact Placement of Titles within a Clip

What if you want the title to appear at a specific point within a clip—for example, exactly 10 seconds into the clip? Because iMovie 2 only allows you to add a title to the beginning of a clip, you need to make your desired spot in the clip the beginning of a clip. You achieve this by splitting the clip into two.

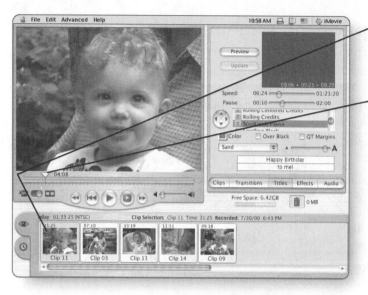

1. **Click** on the **clip** in which you want your title to appear. The clip will be selected.

2. **Press and hold** the **mouse button** on the playhead in the Monitor window and **drag** the **playhead** to the time at which you want the title to appear.

3. **Release** the **mouse button**. The playhead will be located where you released the mouse button.

4. **Click** on **Edit**. The Edit menu will appear.

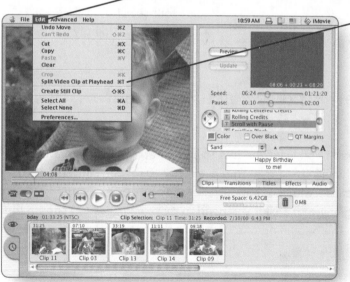

5. **Click** on **Split Video Clip at Playhead**.

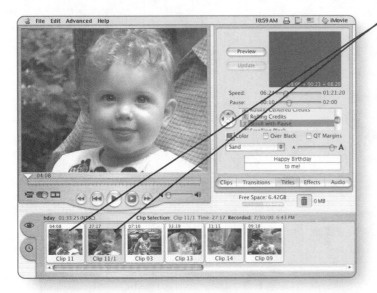

The clip will split into two clips, which will both appear in the Clip Viewer. The second clip is the exact point at which your title will begin, once you add it. You will learn how to add your title in the next section, "Adding a Title to Your iMovie."

Adding a Title to Your iMovie

After you have all of the specs for your titles and credits defined, you just need to add the titles to your production.

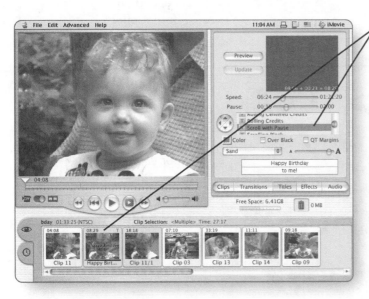

1. Press and hold the **mouse button** on your title selection in the title styles window and **drag** the **title selection** to the clip in the Clip Viewer to which you want to attach it. The clip will move slightly to the right.

2. Release the **mouse button**. The clip to which you attached the title will split into two. The portion of the clip with the title will become a new clip and will have a "T" in the upper-right corner to signify that it is a title clip.

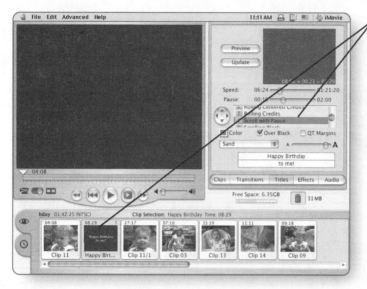

3. If you're placing a title over a black background, **press and hold** the **mouse button** on your title selection in the title styles window and **drag** the **title selection** to the location in the Clip Viewer where you want it to appear.

4. Release the **mouse button**. The title will begin rendering.

TIP

You can add more than one text element to a clip. After adding the Centered Large title to a clip, for example, you can add Subtitle text to the same clip, varying the font color, style, and duration for a different effect.

Changing Your Title

Perhaps you have created a title for your video and, after looking at it, you decide you don't like what you see. Changing a title is a simple process.

1. Click on the **clip** that contains the title. The clip will be selected.

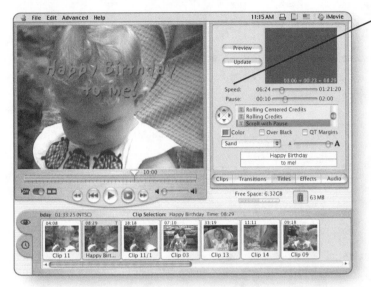

2. Make any **changes** to the font style or color, title style or duration, and so on, following the steps described in this chapter.

3. Click on **Update**. Your changes will take effect.

Deleting Your Title

Suppose that after viewing your movie with its new title, you decide that the title really isn't necessary and you want to get rid of it completely. You can just throw it in the trash.

1. **Press and hold** the **mouse button** on the clip that contains the title you want to discard and **drag** the **title** to the trash can.

2. **Release** the **mouse button**. Your title will be deleted.

8

Audio: Adding Soundtracks, Scores, Sounds, and Narration

Musical scores or soundtracks set the mood for your movies. Adding sound effects and narration also enhances your epic. The best movies have well-balanced audio effects to complement the visuals. Think of how different movies like *Goodfellas* and *Taxi Driver* would be without the voice-over narration, or *Top Gun* and *Pulp Fiction* without the musical soundtracks, or *Star Wars* without sound effects. Effective audio can change the whole complexion of your movies. In this chapter, you'll learn how to:

- Record music from a CD
- Add sound effects
- Add narration
- Crop, delete, and move audio tracks
- Adjust audio levels

Touring the Timeline Viewer and Audio Panel

The Timeline Viewer is the tab with the clock symbol, located behind the Clip Viewer with which you've been working in previous chapters. This is the workspace in which you edit your iMovie's audio. The Audio panel shows the various songs on your CD and allows you to play, record, and add the individual songs. It also houses a number of sound effects and allows you to record a narration.

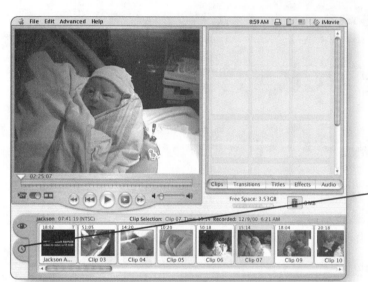

1. Click on the **Timeline Viewer tab**. The Timeline Viewer will appear.

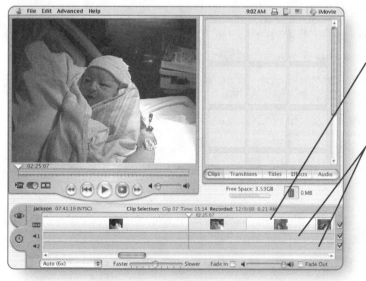

The Timeline Viewer has three tracks:

- The top track is the video track. This track houses the clips and sounds from your video footage.

- The middle and bottom tracks are audio tracks 1 and 2. They house your music, narration, sound effects, and extracted audio from clips.

Other items in the Timeline Viewer, which you'll learn more about as you read this chapter, are as follows:

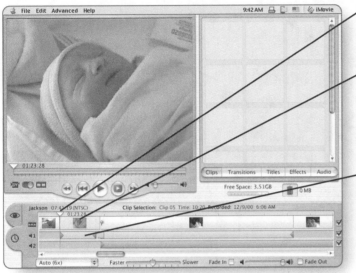

- **Playhead**. The inverted triangle with the line dropping through each track.

- **Video clip with corresponding sound**. An individual audio clip from your camcorder, and its location in your movie.

- **Narration clip**. An individual narration clip that you add, and its location in your movie.

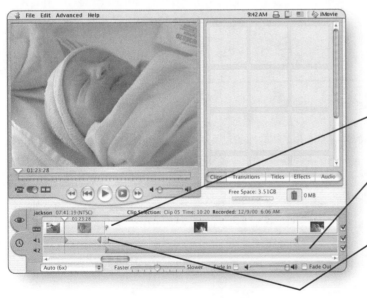

- **Extracted audio clip**. An audio that is extracted from a video clip. It can be moved around or "locked" in place, as you will later learn.

- **Pushpin**. Indicates that audio is locked to the video clip above it.

- **Music clip**. An individual music clip that you add, and its location in your movie.

- **Sound effect clip**. An individual sound effect clip that you add, and its location in your movie.

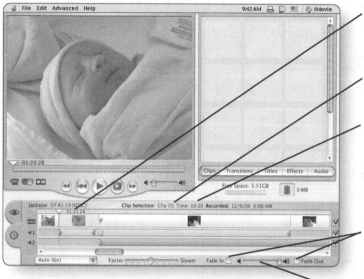

- **Start of clip**. The start time in your movie of the selected audio clip.

- **Name of clip**. The name of the selected audio clip.

- **Length of clip**. The length of the selected audio clip.

- **End of clip**. The stop time in your movie of the selected audio clip.

- **Fade In/Fade Out check boxes**. Allow you to fade your audio clip in or out.

- **Volume slider**. Determines the volume level of clips.

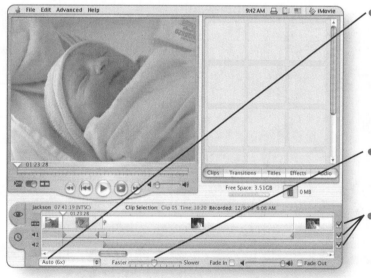

- **Clip zoom level**. Allows you to view more or fewer thumbnail video clips in the top track. The default, or Auto, is 6x. 1x allows you to see all of your video's thumbnail clips on the screen at once.

- **Motion slider**. Allows you to speed up or slow down your clips.

- **Enable/Disable track check boxes**. Allow you to enable or mute the video camera sound track, narration track, or music track.

2. Click on **Audio** in the Design panel. The Audio panel will appear. The Audio panel has the following features:

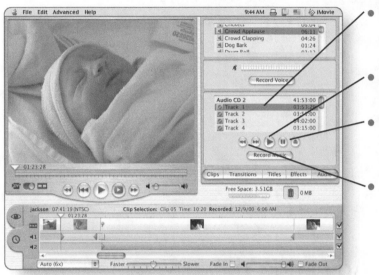

- **Sound track list box**. Lists all of the individual songs on your CD.

- **Play/Stop button**. Plays/stops the selected song or songs.

- **Pause button**. Pauses the playback of the selected song or songs.

- **Previous track/Next track buttons**. Finds the beginning of the next or previous song on the CD.

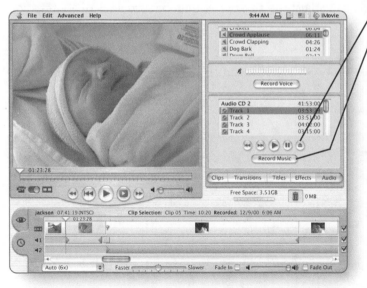

- **Eject button**. Ejects your CD.

- **Record Music button**. Records a song and imports it into the bottom track of the Timeline Viewer.

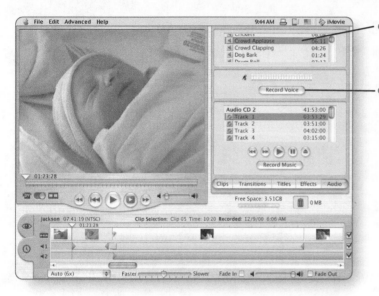

● **Sound effects list box**. Lists the sound effects available to you.

● **Record Voice button**. Records your voice for a narration effect.

Adjusting the Size of Thumbnails

You can adjust the size of the thumbnail images of your audio clips in the video track of the Timeline Viewer, allowing you to see tiny images of all of your individual video clips in the Timeline Viewer at once. You can also turn off the thumbnail images altogether if you like.

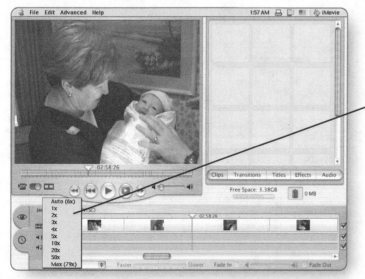

1. Click on the **up and down arrows** next to Auto (6X). A pop-up menu will appear.

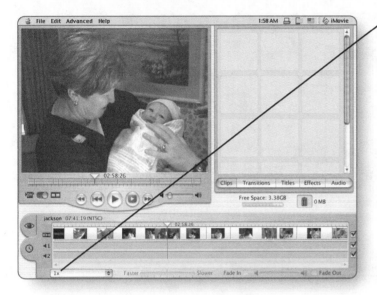

2. **Click** on a **viewing size**. (The lower the number, the more images will appear on the Timeline at once. 1X will show all of your video clips at once on your screen.) The size will be selected.

3. **Click** on **Edit**. The Edit menu will appear.

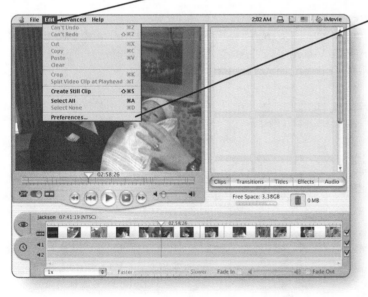

4. **Click** on **Preferences**. The Preferences dialog box will open.

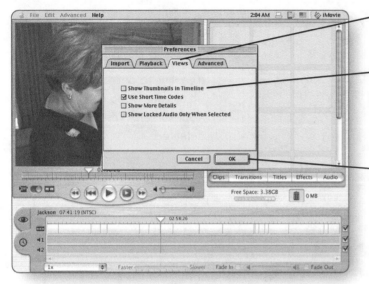

5. Click on the **Views tab**. The Views tab will appear.

6. Click on the **Show Thumbnails in Timeline check box** to remove the checkmark. The checkmark will be removed.

7. Click on **OK**. The thumbnails will be turned off in your Timeline.

Adding Music from an Audio CD

One of the simplest ways to include your favorite songs in your movies is to pop in a CD and import the song into the Timeline Viewer in iMovie 2. You can add entire songs or portions of your favorite hits.

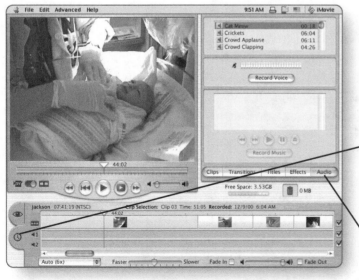

Adding a Song from a CD

Adding a song from a CD to your movie is a simple drag-and-drop procedure.

1. Click on the **Timeline Viewer tab**, if you haven't already done so. The Timeline Viewer will appear.

2. Click on **Audio**. The Audio panel will appear.

3. **Insert** your **CD** into the CD-ROM drive. The songs will appear in the list box in the Audio panel after a few seconds.

4. **Press and hold** the **mouse button** on the scroll bar in the scroll box and **drag up or down** to search for your song.

NOTE

iMovie doesn't reveal the actual names of the songs on your CD. If you can't figure out which song is which, just click on a track number and then click Play. The song will play, and you will know what track number it is.

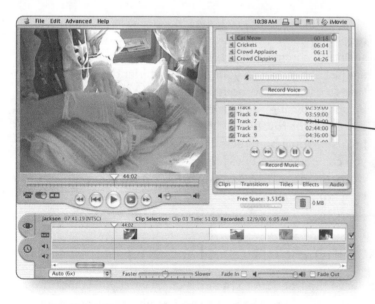

5. **Press and hold** the **mouse button** on the song you want to add and **drag** the **song** to audio track 1 or 2 in the Timeline Viewer.

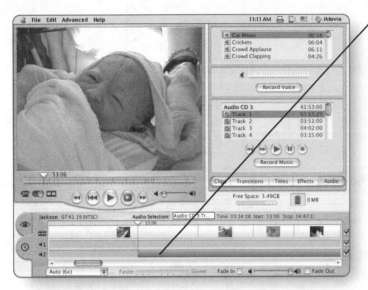

6. **Release** the **mouse button**. The song will import from the CD and appear in the track after a few seconds.

NOTE

There are copyright law issues to keep in mind when recording audio from CDs. As long as you are not selling or commercially releasing your movie and you are just showing it to your family and friends, you are safe to use audio without permissions. You can also pick up some royalty-free music, or buyout music, by searching for *royalty-free music* or *buyout music* in your browser. You'll be directed to some Web sites where you can pay a one-time fee for tunes and not have to worry about getting into any trouble from using others' copyrighted music.

Adding a Portion of a Song

You have the freedom to record exactly what you want from your CD. You are not limited to adding an entire song. Use the Record Music button to record just a portion of a song for your movie.

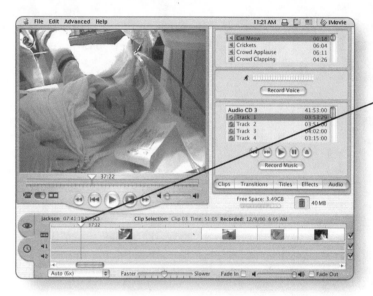

1. **Repeat steps 1 through 4** in the previous section, "Adding a Song from a CD."

2. **Press and hold** the **mouse button** on the playhead and drag it to the point in the Timeline Viewer where you want the music to begin recording.

3. **Release** the **mouse button**. This is the point where your music will start recording.

TIP
Press the Home key on your keyboard to immediately move to the beginning of your clips.

NOTE
You'll learn more about editing your audio clips later in this chapter, in the "Editing Audio Clips" section. For now, you'll focus on just adding the music to your movie.

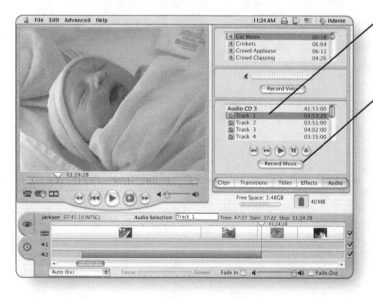

4. **Click** on the **song** you want to insert into your movie. The track will be selected.

5. **Click** on **Record Music**. The track will begin playing and recording in the music track in the Timeline Viewer. The video footage will also play in the Monitor window as the song records. The Record Music button will become a Stop button.

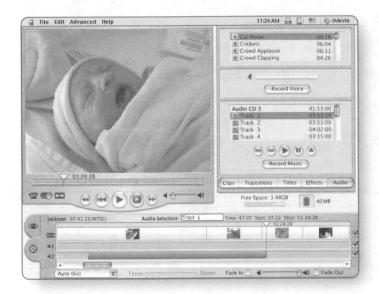

6. **Click** on **Stop** to stop recording. The track will cease recording.

Adding Sound Effects

iMovie contains a handful of sound effects in its Effects panel. You can become the post-production sound effect artist for your movie by introducing footsteps, broken glass, rain falling, and other sounds. Add sound effects in either the narration track or the music track.

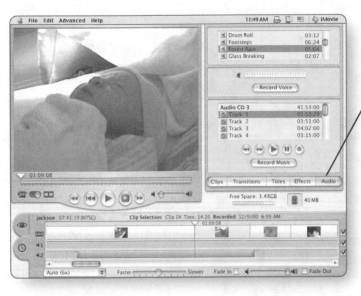

1. **Click** on **Audio** in the Design panel, if you haven't already done so. The Audio panel will appear.

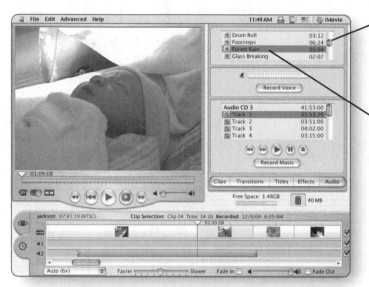

2. Press and hold the **mouse button** on the scroll bar and **drag up and down** to scroll through the list of effects.

3. Click on a **sound effect**. A sampling of the sound effect will play.

4. Press and hold the **mouse button** on the sound and **drag** the **sound** down to your desired location on either audio track in the Timeline Viewer. An outline of the sound will appear as you drag it, and a yellow line will appear on the track to indicate the approximate placement of the sound effect.

5. Release the **mouse button**. The sound effect will be represented by a blue square in the audio track.

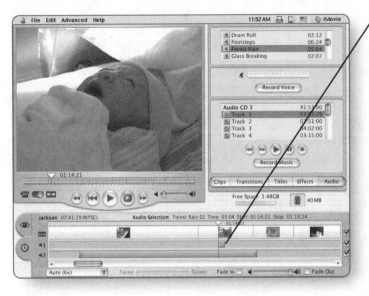

6. Click and hold the **mouse button** on the blue square and **drag it** left or right to the position where you want the sound effect to go. The playhead, its vertical line, and the time counter will appear as you drag.

7. Release the **mouse button**. The sound effect will be positioned where you want it.

TIP

To precisely locate the sound effect, click on the blue square to select it, and then press the left and right arrows on your keyboard to move frame-by-frame left or right.

Adding Voice-Over or Narration

Narrate or add voice-over to tell the story of your movie or to reveal behind-the-scenes information to your audience. iMacs and PowerBooks have built-in microphones, which you'll need to record your voice. Ever wonder what that little oval hole at the top of your iMac computer screen is? That's the internal microphone. You can also use an external microphone to accomplish this task. Power Macs come with an external microphone. This section will focus on using the internal mike.

1. Click on the **Apple icon**. The Apple menu will appear.

2. Click on **Control Panels**. The Control Panels menu will appear.

3. Click on **Sound**. The Sound dialog box will open.

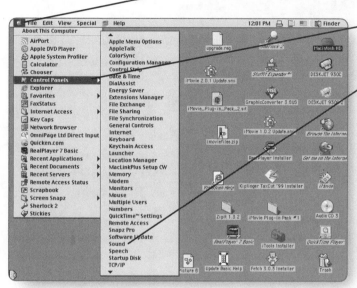

4. Click on **Input** in the left list box. Input will be selected.

5. Click on **Built-in** in the Choose a device for sound input list box. Built-in will be selected.

6. Click on the **up and down arrows** to the right of the Input Source list box. A list of input options will appear.

7. Click on **Built-in Mic**. Built-in Mic will be selected.

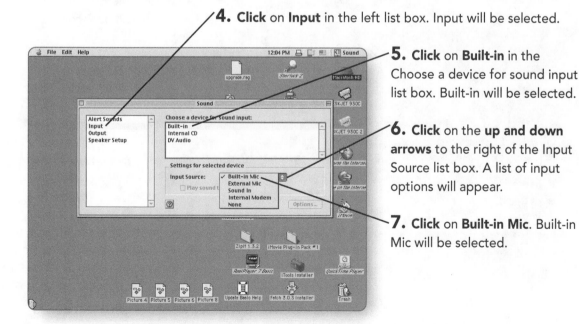

8. **Close** the **Sound dialog box**.

9. **Open iMovie** and **open** the **movie project** to which you want to add your voice. The project will open.

10. **Drag** the **playhead** to the point in the Timeline Viewer where you want your narration to begin. The playhead will be positioned.

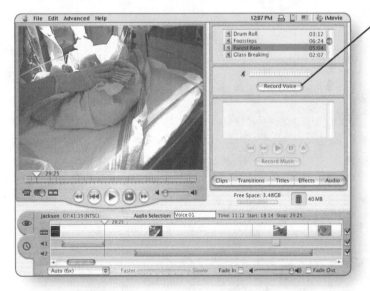

11. **Click** on **Record Voice** and **speak** into the **microphone**. Your narration will be recorded.

12. **Click** on **Stop** when you are done recording. Your narration will be complete.

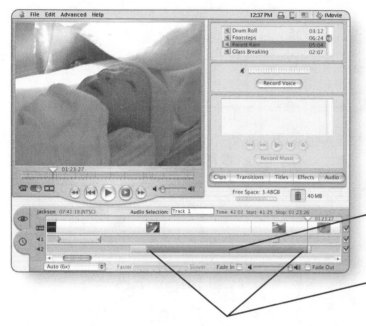

Editing Audio Clips

If you want to position a song to play over a certain portion or duration of your movie, you can crop the music exactly at the desired location and then fade it in and out to polish it up.

1. **Click** on an **audio clip** in the Timeline Viewer. The clip will be selected.

2. **Press and hold** the **mouse button** on the crop markers (triangles) at both ends of the clip and **drag** the **triangles** to the desired locations.

3. **Release** the **mouse button**. The crop markers will be positioned.

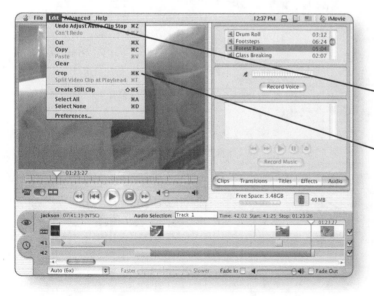

4. **Click** on **Edit**. The Edit menu will appear.

5. **Click** on **Crop**. The audio clip will be cropped where you indicated.

TIP

For more precise cropping, click on the beginning or ending triangle and press the left and right arrow keys to move a single frame at a time.

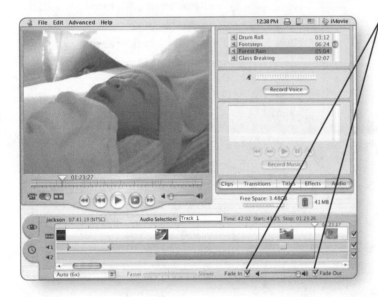

6. **Click** on the **Fade In and Fade Out check boxes** to insert check marks. The music clip will fade in at the beginning and fade out at the end.

Moving an Audio Clip

You can move narration, music, and sound effect clips to different places in the Timeline Viewer. These audio clips can even overlap, and iMovie will play all of the sounds simultaneously.

1. **Press and hold** the **mouse button** on an audio clip you want to move and **drag** the **clip** to the desired position. The playhead and time counter will appear as you drag.

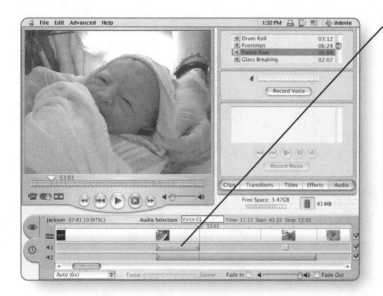

2. Release the **mouse button**. The audio clip will now be in its new position.

TIP

Remember, you can use the left and right arrow keys on the keyboard for more precise positioning.

Accessing Audio Clip Information and Renaming an Audio Clip

By double-clicking on an audio clip, you can access that clip's vital information, just as you did with video clips. While in the information box, you can see what type of file the clip is and its size, and you can give your audio clips distinguishable names so that you can easily remember what they are. You can also fade the clip's audio in and out from the Clip Info box; doing so will be discussed later in this chapter.

1. Double-click on an **audio clip** you want to rename. The Clip Info dialog box will open.

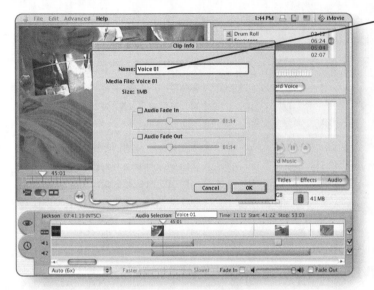

2. Click and drag the **mouse pointer** on the current clip name in the Name text box. The name will be selected.

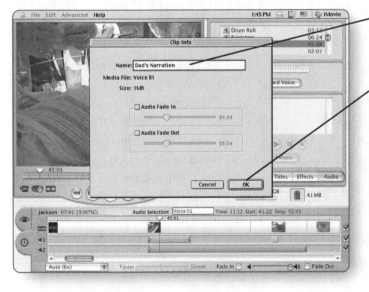

3. Type a new **name** for the clip. The new name will appear in the text box.

4. Click on **OK**. The clip will be renamed.

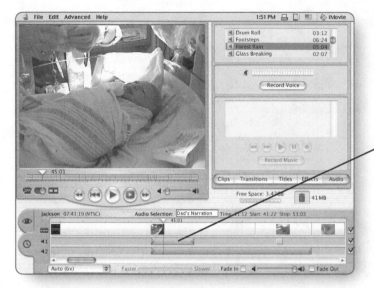

Deleting an Audio Track

Deleting an audio track is easy, too. Simply follow these steps.

1. **Click** on the **music track, sound effect, or narration clip** in the Timeline Viewer. The audio track for that item will be selected.

2. **Press** the **Delete key**. The audio track for that item will be deleted.

Adjusting Audio Levels

You can adjust the levels of sound in your video footage to a mere hum of background noise while your musical soundtrack plays, or reduce your musical soundtrack to a low harmony while the sound from your video footage dominates the scene. You can also mute the sound from your video footage altogether, and even fade your musical score in and out.

Adjusting the Volume of a Clip or Clips

You can adjust your computer's overall volume level for audio playback, and you can adjust the volume of individual video camera sound clips, music clips, or narration sound clips.

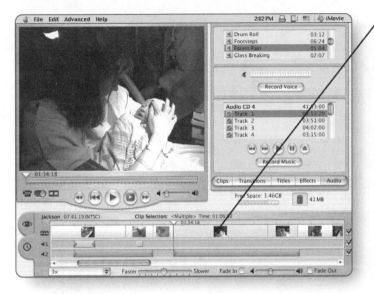

1. **Click** on an **audio clip or series of audio clips** in the Timeline Viewer. The clip or clips will be selected.

NOTE
Press and hold the Shift key as you click to select multiple clips.

2. **Press and hold** the **mouse button** on the volume slider and **drag** the **slider** left to decrease the volume or right to increase the volume. This will adjust the volume of the audio track or tracks you selected.

TIP
Drag the slider all the way to the left to mute the sound of your selected audio clip or clips. You might want to do this to a video clip that has some bad sound, and then turn up the volume on a music track to give the video clip some sort of audio.

Adjusting the Volume within a Single Clip

Is there an annoying sound within a single clip that you want to reduce? To control the volume level within a single clip, you need to split the clip at the point where you want the sound level to vary, and then adjust the volume at that point.

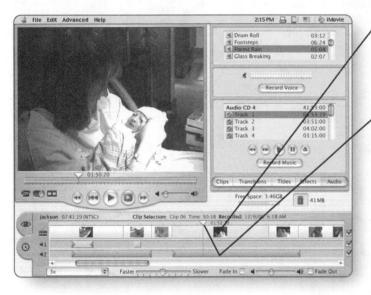

1. **Click** on the **video thumbnail clip** whose volume you want to adjust. The clip will be selected.

2. **Press and hold** the **mouse button** on the playhead and **drag** the **playhead** to the point where you want to adjust the volume.

3. **Release** the **mouse button**. The playhead will be positioned.

4. **Click** on **Edit**. The Edit menu will appear.

5. **Click** on **Split Video Clip at Playhead**. The clip will be split into two new clips.

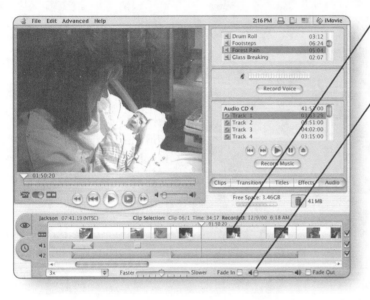

6. **Click** on the **second of the two new clips**. The clip will be selected.

7. **Press and hold** the **mouse button** on the volume slider and **drag** the **slider** left to reduce the sound level.

8. **Release** the **mouse button**. The sound level will be adjusted.

Muting Audio Tracks

You can get rid of your video footage's background sounds altogether. You can also completely mute your recordings in the narration track or music track, or both.

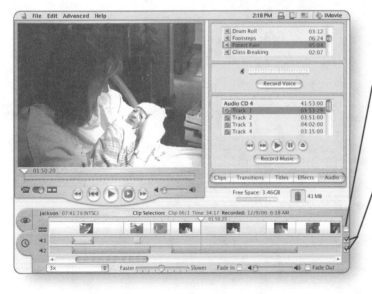

1. **Click** on one or more of the following **check boxes** to remove a check mark:

- Removing the check mark in the check box to the right of the video camera sound track will mute the video camera's sound.

- Removing the check mark in the check box to the right of either audio track 1 or 2 will mute the music, narration, or sound effects clips in that track.

Fading Your Recording In and Out

You can polish your movie by fading your music recordings in and out of your scenes. This is especially helpful when you are using only part of a song in a single clip or series of clips, or if your song is longer than the length of your movie.

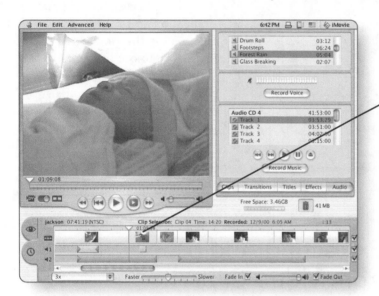

1. Double-click on an **audio clip** that you want to fade in or out. The Clip Info dialog box will open.

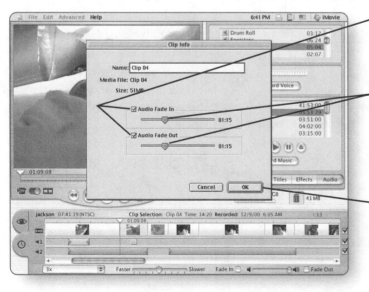

2. Click on the **check boxes** next to Audio Fade In and Audio Fade Out to insert check marks.

3. Press and hold the **mouse button** on the fade duration sliders and **drag them** to set the speed at which your audio clip will fade in and out.

4. Click on **OK**. Your fades will be set.

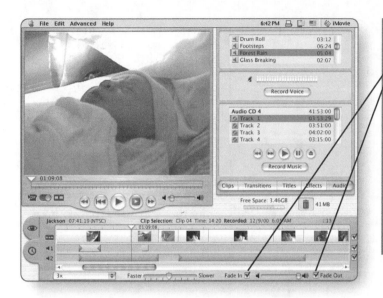

You can also select the clip to which you want to add fades and click on the Fade In and Fade Out check boxes in the Timeline Viewer to get the same effect. But if you use this method, you cannot adjust the duration of these fades like you did in Step 3 of this section.

Extracting Audio from Video Clips

Got a great sound bite in one video clip that you want to use in another video clip? Suppose you have the Best Man's speech in one long video clip that you want to play over a different scene of the newlyweds. You can extract that audio from the first clip and attach it to the clip of the newlyweds.

1. Click on the **video clip** that has audio you want to extract. The clip will be selected.

2. Click on **Advanced**. The Advanced menu will appear.

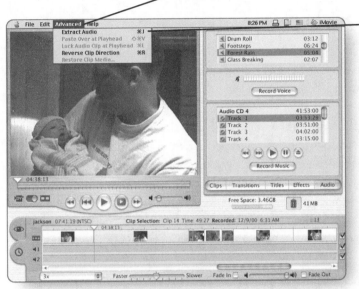

3. Click on **Extract Audio**. The audio will be extracted from the video clip and inserted on the middle audio track in the Timeline Viewer.

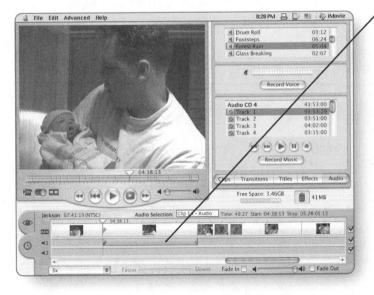

By extracting the video clip's audio, iMovie is actually copying the audio, placing it on the audio track, and muting the audio from that video clip. Notice the pushpins in the video track and the extracted audio track. Those pushpins show that the audio is locked in position with that video clip. If you want to move the extracted audio to a different location away from its original video clip, you must "unlock" it, which you'll learn how to do in the next section.

Locking and Unlocking Audio and Video Clips

Locking an audio clip with a video clip means that the audio clip stays in sync with the video clip. If you want to keep these two together, locking them is an important task. When you are sliding clips around in the Timeline Viewer, or cutting and pasting new video clips here and there, audio and video clips are shifting all around. If you lock the audio and the video, they will always stay in sync no matter how much shifting goes on in the Timeline Viewer. On the other hand, there are times (like the hypothetical situation discussed in the previous section) when you want to unlock the audio from the video and move it to be in sync with another area of your production.

Unlocking Audio from Video Clips

You should still have "locked" video and audio after doing the extracting exercise from the section "Extracting Audio from Video Clips." If you don't, go ahead and extract some audio from a video clip as described in that section. Remember, locked clips are represented by pushpins.

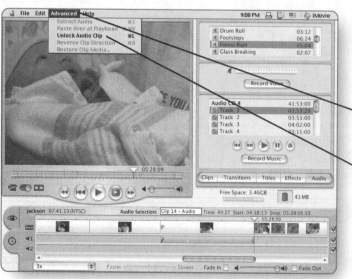

1. **Click** on the **audio clip** that you want to unlock from the video clip. The clip will be selected.

2. **Click** on **Advanced**. The Advanced menu will appear.

3. **Click** on **Unlock Audio Clip**. The pushpins will disappear and the audio clip will be available to move independently from the video clip.

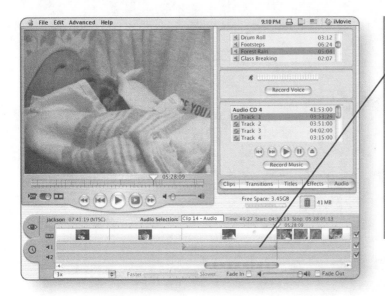

TIP

When you move this unlocked, extracted audio clip to its new location, make sure you turn down the volume of the video clip that will now correspond to this new audio or else you will hear the audio of both jumbled together.

Locking Audio to Video Clips

On the flip side, suppose you have an audio clip that you want to stay put at a particular spot in your video. This is when you lock the audio.

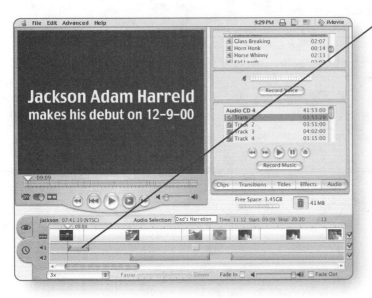

1. **Click** on the **audio clip** that you want to lock to video. The clip will be selected.

2. **Press and hold** the **mouse button** on the clip and **drag it** to where you want the beginning of the audio clip to lock with the video clip. The playhead will represent the exact location where the video and audio clips will lock.

3. **Click** on **Advanced**. The Advanced menu will appear.

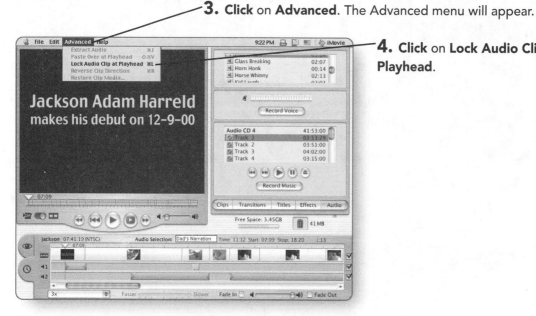

4. **Click** on **Lock Audio Clip at Playhead**.

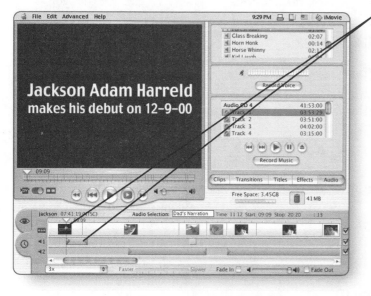

Pushpins will appear and the video and audio will be locked together.

Now the audio clip and video clip cannot be accidentally separated while you continue to make edits to your production in the Timeline.

Insert Video-Clip Editing

Insert video-clip, or "cutaway," editing simply means inserting a video clip inside another video clip. This process overlays one video clip on another, while keeping the original video clip's audio intact. Think of cutaways on TV or in the movies. Suppose you're taping an interview with two people. You want to film the interviewee answering the interviewer's question, but you also want to see the reaction of the interviewer while the interviewee is still talking. This is done using the Paste Over command. Another example might be inserting close-up footage of a handsome new baby boy within video clips of proud parents and grandparents, without losing the sounds of oohs and aahs from the original video clip.

1. Click on a **clip** that you want to insert into another clip. The clip will be selected.

2. Click on **Edit**. The Edit menu will appear.

3. Click on **Copy**. The clip will be copied.

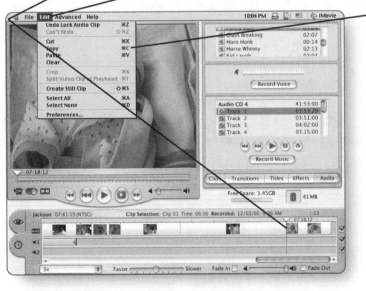

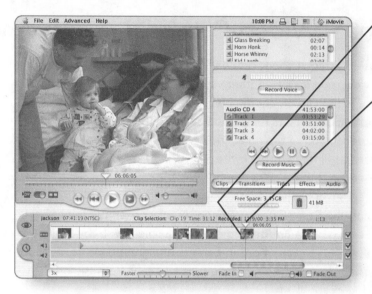

4. Click on the **clip** into which you want the copied clip to be pasted. The clip will be selected.

5. Drag the **playhead** to the location within the clip where you want the copied clip to be pasted.

6. Click on **Advanced**. The Advanced menu will appear.

7. Click on **Paste Over at Playhead**.

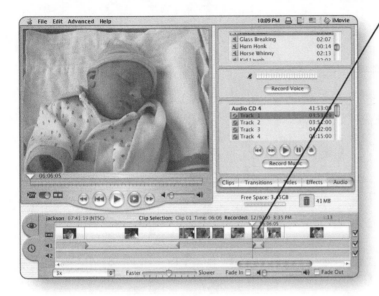

The copied clip will be pasted into the video clip.

The inserted clip will lose its audio, and the original clip's audio will play throughout.

Expanding Your Sound Effect and Looping Music Library

You can add more sound effects and looping music files to your iMovie arsenal by inserting them into the Sound Effects folder, which can be found in the Resources folder within the iMovie folder on your hard drive. Apple's Web site has a nice collection of sound effects and looping music.

1. Go to **Apple's iMovie page** (http://www.apple.com/imovie).

2. Scroll down and **click** on **Enhance**. The Enhance page will appear.

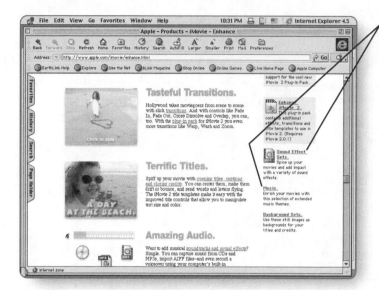

3. Scroll down and **click** on **Sound Effect Sets or Music**. The library of sounds effects or looping music will appear.

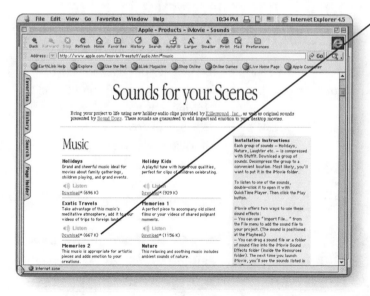

4. Click on **Download** for the sample you want. The set will download to your desktop.

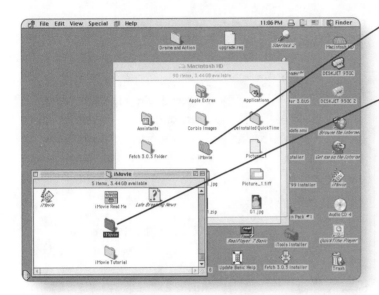

5. Double-click on the **iMovie folder** on your hard drive. The iMovie folder will open.

6. Double-click on the **second iMovie folder**. The second iMovie folder will open.

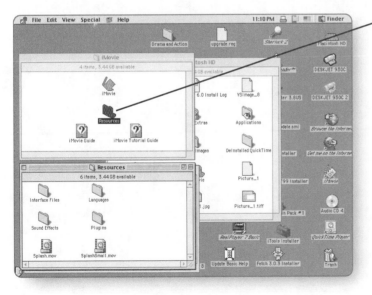

7. Double-click on the **Resources folder**. The Resources folder will open.

8. Double-click on the **folder** of sound effects or music that you downloaded. The folder will open.

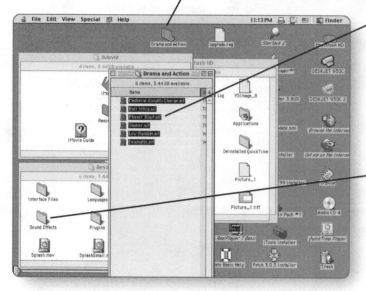

9. Press and hold the **mouse button** down, **highlight** all of the **sound files** that you downloaded, and **drag them** to the Sound Effects folder. The Sound Effects folder will be highlighted.

10. Release the **mouse button**. The new sounds will be available the next time you run iMovie 2.

9

Special Effects

iMovie 2 allows you to add some interesting touches to your footage. Make Junior's home-run trot more dramatic with slow-motion effects. Or, speed it up for that 1920s Babe Ruth look. Give your films a noir feel with black-and-white or sepia tones. Improve bad lighting in your footage by adjusting the brightness. Or, add some crazy mirror images or ghost trails to your horror flick. Although most of the effects in iMovie 2 can really enhance your projects, others are just for fun and should probably be used sparingly. In this chapter, you'll learn how to:

- Use slow motion and fast motion
- Play video clips backwards
- Distort video images
- Alter color, brightness, and hue

Creating Slow-Motion and Fast-Motion Effects

Two of the more effective techniques used by many filmmakers are slow-motion and fast-motion montages. Think of the slow-motion opening credit scene of *Reservoir Dogs*, or the fast motion used in Martin Scorsese films such as *Bringing Out the Dead*. Or, as in *Lock, Stock, and Two Smoking Barrels*, a combination of slow and fast motion, if you can believe it.

1. **Click** on the **Timeline Viewer tab**. The Timeline Viewer will appear.

2. **Click** on the **clip** you want to enhance with slow or fast motion. The clip will be selected.

3. **Press and hold** the **mouse button** on the motion slider and **drag it** left to cause the video clip to go slower, or right to go faster.

4. **Release** the **mouse button**. The motion speed will be set.

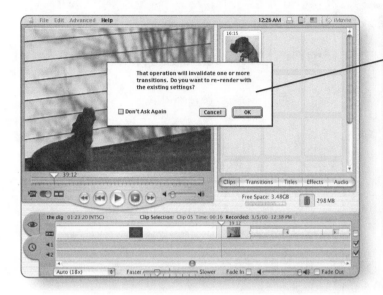

NOTE

If you have a transition attached to a clip to which you want to add a slow- or fast-motion effect, iMovie 2 will display a warning box telling you that the transition will be invalidated. If you don't mind losing the transition, click on OK.

Playing Video Clips Backwards

iMovie 2 can take your clips and reverse them. That's right, Junior can make his home-run trot backwards. This might sound like an effect that is just for fun and will only add some

silliness to your productions, but it actually has some usefulness. If you only have a zoom-out or pan-left shot, but you need a zoom-in or pan-right shot, the reverse-clip trick comes in handy.

1. Click on the **clip** you want to run backwards. The clip will be selected.

2. Click on **Advanced**. The Advanced menu will appear.

3. Click on **Reverse Clip Direction**. The clip will be reversed.

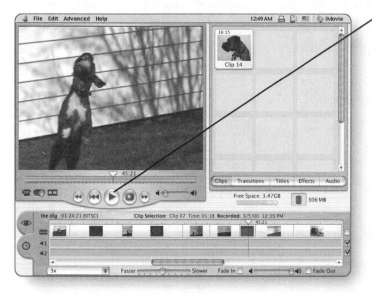

4. Click on the **Play button**. You will see your clip run in reverse.

Distorting Video Clips in the Effects Panel

A number of special effects in the Effects panel will help you warp your video footage. Make sure you have downloaded and installed the plug-in pack that you learned about in Chapter 6, "Adding Stylish Transitions." This pack includes some extra effects that you can use.

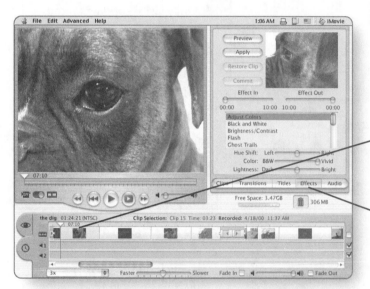

1. Click on the **clip** to which you want to apply a special effect. The clip will be selected.

2. Click on **Effects**. The Effects panel will appear.

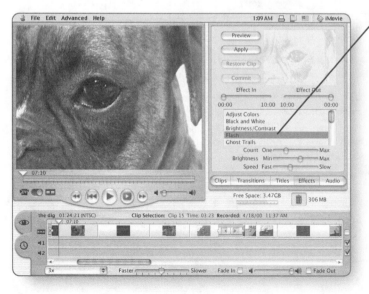

3. Click on **Flash**. The Flash details will appear and a quick preview of the effect will appear in the small preview window. Choosing Flash adds bright-light flashes to your video clip.

Notice the following in the panel:

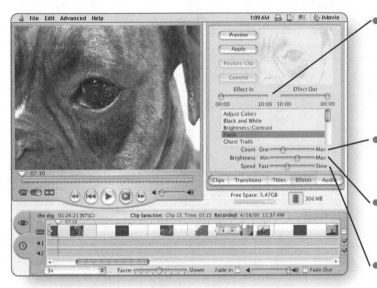

- **Effect In/Effect Out**. Drag these sliders to determine how much time will elapse in the clip before the effect is fully visible and when the effect will no longer be visible.

- **Count**. Drag this slider to determine the number of flashes in the effect.

- **Brightness**. Drag this slider to determine the magnitude of the brightness of the effect.

- **Speed**. Drag this slider to determine the speed at which the flash or flashes occur.

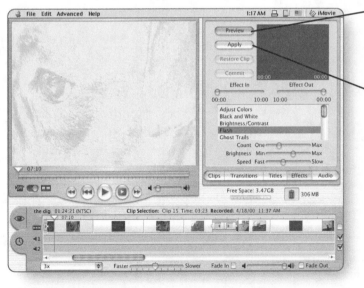

4. **Click** on **Preview**. Your effect will play in the Monitor window.

5. **Click** on **Apply**. Your effect will be rendered.

6. Click on **one** of the following:

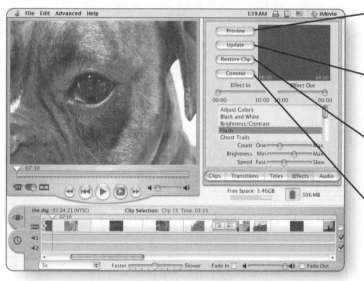

- **Preview**. Select this if you want to see another preview of your effect.

- **Update**. Select this if you want to change the effect on this clip to another effect.

- **Restore Clip**. Select this if you want to restore your clip to its original state.

- **Commit**. Select this if you want to permanently apply the effect to your clip. If you select this option, you cannot restore your clip to its original state.

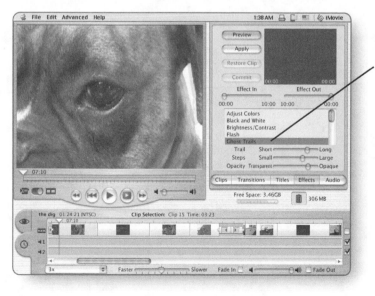

Other effects that distort your video are as follows:

- **Ghost Trails**. This adds a psychedelic blurring-and-trailing effect to your subjects as they move.

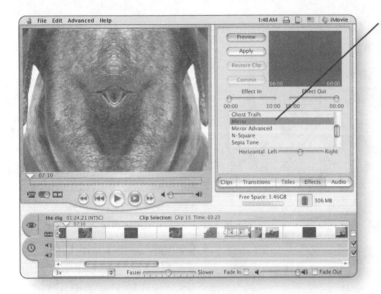

- **Mirror**. This gives your subject a funhouse-mirror effect.

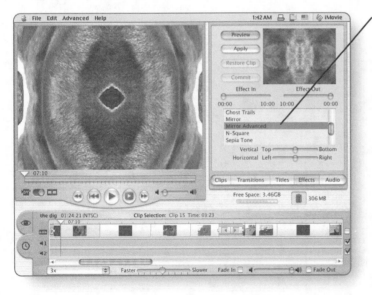

- **Mirror Advanced**. This takes the Mirror effect a step further.

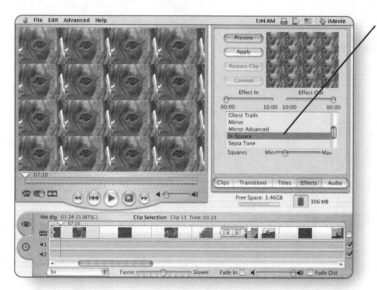

- **N-Square**. This breaks your video up into several small squares, almost as though you were looking through a fly's eyes.

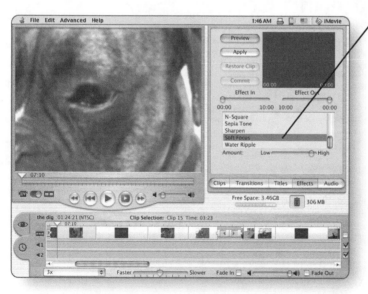

- **Soft Focus**. This adds a blurry effect to your video.

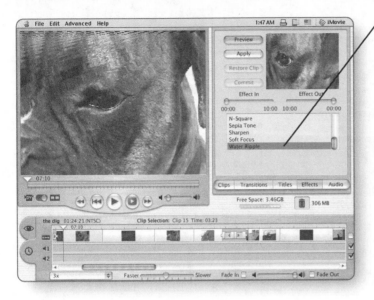

- **Water Ripple**. This makes your video look as though you filmed it under water.

Most of these effects have slightly different details regarding how to adjust them to fit your particular needs. Just toy with whatever slider bars appear to create the effect you desire.

Altering Color, Brightness, and Hue

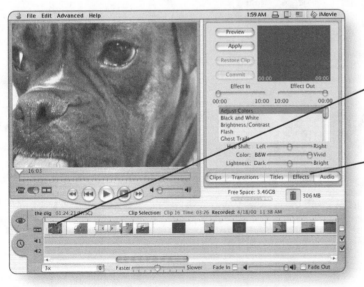

Other effects in the Effects panel deal with color, brightness, and hue.

1. Click on the **clip** to which you want to add the special effect. The clip will be selected.

2. Click on **Effects**, if you haven't already selected it. The Effects panel will appear.

3. Click on **Adjust Colors**. The Adjust Colors details will appear and a quick preview will play in the small preview window in the Effects panel. Adjust Colors allows you to do just that—adjust the colors in your footage.

Notice the following in the panel:

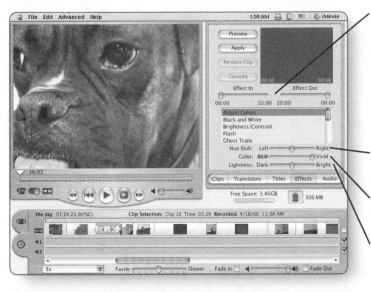

- **Effect In/Effect Out**. Drag these sliders to determine how much time will elapse in your video clip before the effect is fully visible and when the effect will no longer be visible.

- **Hue Shift**. Drag the slider to adjust the hue in your footage.

- **Color**. Drag the slider to adjust the color in your footage.

- **Lightness**. Drag the slider to adjust the brightness of your footage.

4. Click on **Preview**. Your effects will preview in the Monitor window.

5. Click on **Apply**. Your effects will be applied to your video clip.

6. Click on **one** of the following:

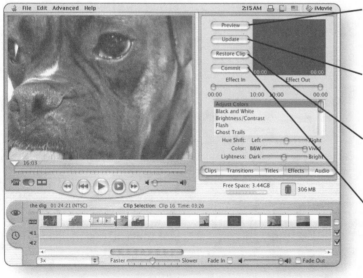

- **Preview**. Select this to see another preview of your effect.

- **Update**. Select this to change the effect on this clip to another effect.

- **Restore Clip**. Select this to restore the clip to its original state.

- **Commit**. Select this to permanently apply the effect to your clip. After you commit, you cannot restore the clip to its original state.

Other effects that adjust color, brightness, and hue are as follows:

- **Black and White**. This, obviously, makes your clips black and white.

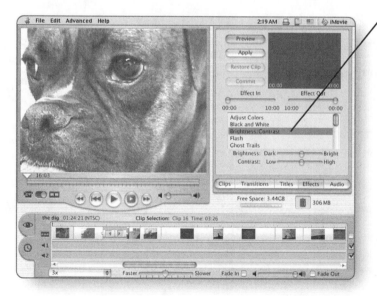

- **Brightness/Contrast**. This controls the brightness and contrast of your footage.

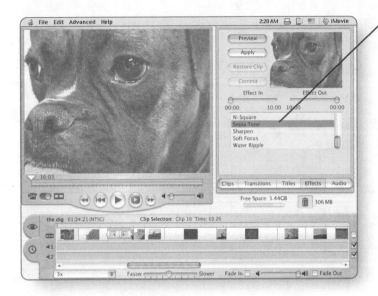

- **Sepia Tone**. This gives your video clips a sepia effect, like film from an earlier era.

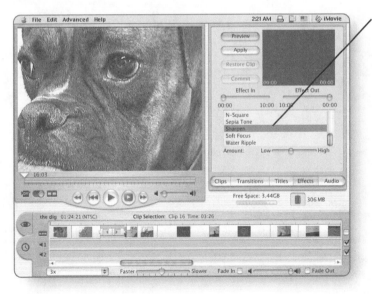

- **Sharpen**. This sharpens or dulls the images in your video clips.

Most of these effects have slightly different details regarding how to adjust them to your particular needs. Just toy with whatever slider bars appear to create the effect you desire.

Using Special Effects to Your Advantage

Experiment with the different effects to create a mood for your production. For example, open your masterpiece in black and white and gradually fade into color. Or, start out with the Soft Focus effect to blur your beginning scene, and then bring your players into focus as your movie rolls on.

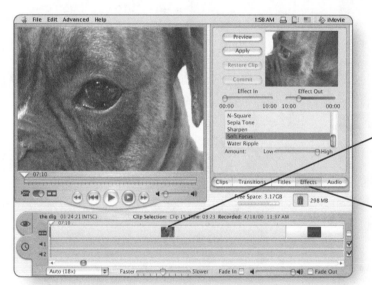

1. **Click** on the **opening clip** of your movie. The clip will be selected.

2. **Click** on **Effects**, if it isn't already selected. The Effects panel will appear.

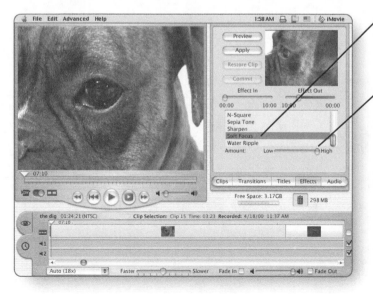

3. **Click** on **Soft Focus**. The Soft Focus effect will be selected.

4. **Drag** the **Amount slider** all the way to the higher end. This will blur the beginning of your clip to its maximum amount.

5. **Adjust** the **Effect In/Effect Out sliders** to set the effect to occur at the very beginning of the clip and end midway through the clip. The effect will be set.

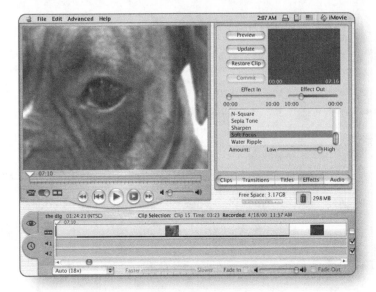

This will allow your movie to begin with a cool, fuzzy beginning montage and gradually come into focus to introduce your setting or characters. Try out some of the other effects to see if you can animate your movies in this way.

10

Compressing and Exporting Your Movies

Now that you've finished your masterpiece, you need to prepare it for presentation. After all, if your movie is not in a format that your audience can view, what good is it? Perhaps you want to display it on videotape, send it as an e-mail attachment, place it on a Web site, or burn it onto a CD. To make use of these formats, you must know how to compress and export your movies. In this chapter, you'll learn how to:

- Save your iMovie
- Make a copy of your iMovie
- Export your movie to a camera
- Make a copy on VHS tape
- Export your movie to QuickTime
- Use the QuickTime Player
- Import QuickTime clips into your iMovies

Saving Your iMovie

Before you export your movie, you need to save it. You wouldn't want to lose any of your hard work if a problem were to occur during the exporting process.

1. Click on **File**. The File menu will appear.

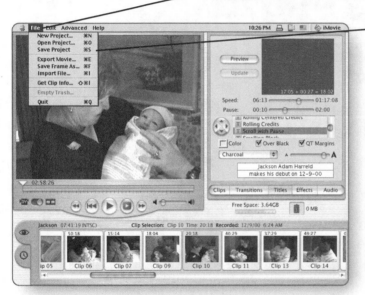

2. Click on **Save Project**. The movie will be saved.

> ### NOTE
> You already gave your project a name and saved it to a particular folder, so you won't be asked to name your movie or save it to a folder again. You are simply making the final save of all the edits and special effects you have recently applied to your project. See the following section, "Making a Copy of Your iMovie," to learn about saving another version of the same movie.

Making a Copy of Your iMovie

Because iMovie does not have a traditional Save As command, you need to take a different approach to saving a copy of your movie project. If you want to make changes to a movie project while keeping a copy of the original version, make a copy of the project file on your hard drive and then make your edits to the duplicate version of the movie.

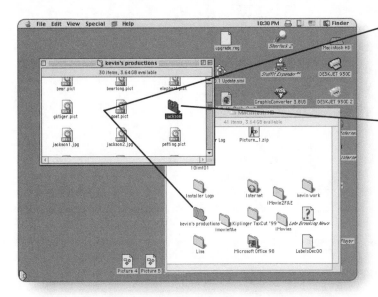

1. Double-click on the **folder** that contains the movie you want to copy. The folder will open.

2. Double-click on the **movie** you want to copy. The movie file and Media folder will appear.

3. Click on the **movie file**. The movie file will be selected.

4. Click on **File**. The File menu will appear.

5. Click on **Duplicate**. Your movie files will begin to duplicate.

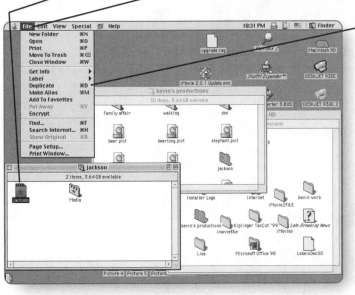

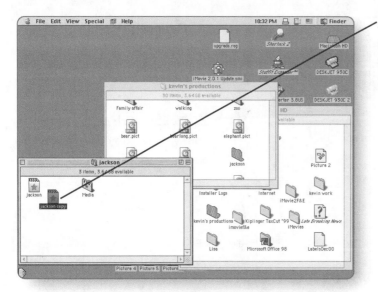

After the duplication process is complete, a copy of the movie will appear next to the original movie file.

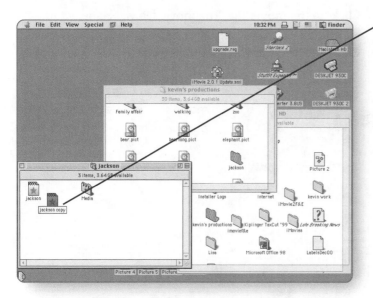

6. Click on the **name** of the copy. The name will be highlighted.

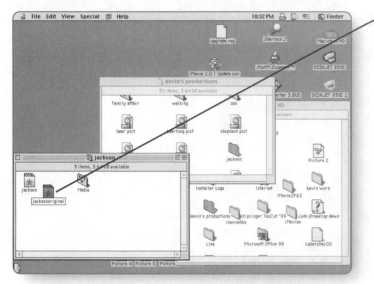

7. Type a new **name** for the copied version.

Exporting Your Movie to Your Camera

You are now ready to export your finished product. One venue of exportation is your DV tape. This allows you to create a library of your edited movies on tape. iMovies take up a tremendous amount of hard drive space, so this is a great way to collect your masterpieces without soaking up your computer's precious space.

1. Turn on your **video camera**, **connect it** to your computer via the FireWire port, and **set** your **camcorder** to VTR/VCR mode.

TIP

Make sure your DV tape is cued to where you want your finished movie to be located. Using a tape dedicated only to your finished iMovies is a nice touch.

---

2. Click on **File**. The File menu will appear.

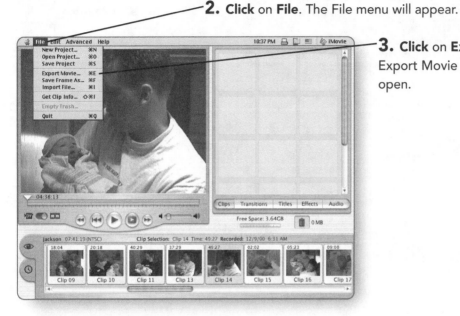

3. Click on **Export Movie**. The Export Movie dialog box will open.

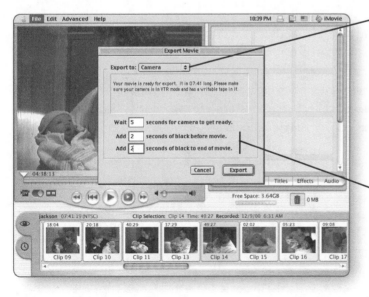

4. Click on the **up and down arrows** to the right of the Export to box. Two export options will appear.

5. Click on **Camera**, if it isn't already selected. The export option will be set to Camera.

6. Type the **duration** of black space you want added to the beginning and to the end of your movie. This gives you a buffer so that your movies don't begin abruptly when played, or end abruptly when completed.

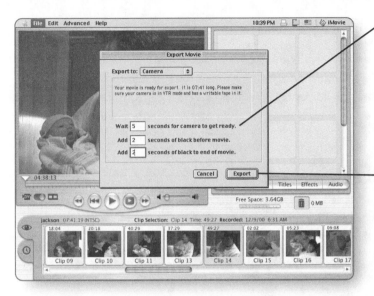

7. **Type** the **amount of time** in seconds you want to allow for your camera to get ready for the export. This gives your camera the time it needs to be ready before iMovie starts exporting your movie.

8. Click on **Export**. The movie will play in the Monitor window as it exports to your camera.

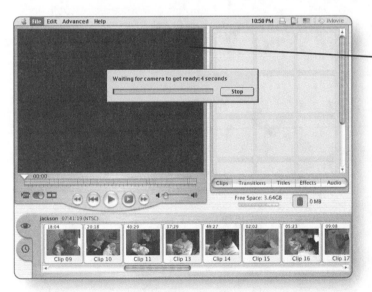

NOTE

The footage might appear grainy as it plays in the Monitor window during exportation. It will not appear this way on your DV tape.

9. Rewind the **tape** in your video camera and **play back** your **masterpiece**.

Making a Copy on VHS Tape

Some of your friends or relatives might not have entered the digital video age yet. For these folks, you might need to copy your movies onto a traditional VHS tape. Unfortunately, you cannot export your iMovie from your Mac straight to a VHS tape. But you can export your iMovie to DV tape and then copy the DV tape to VHS tape.

Make sure the DV tape with your finished iMovie is cued up in your camcorder and you have a blank VHS tape in your VCR. Connect your camcorder to your VCR with A/V connecting cables. These cables usually come with your camcorder.

Make sure you connect the A/V cable to the LINE IN input on your VCR. Check with your camcorder manual if you have trouble connecting your camcorder to your VCR.

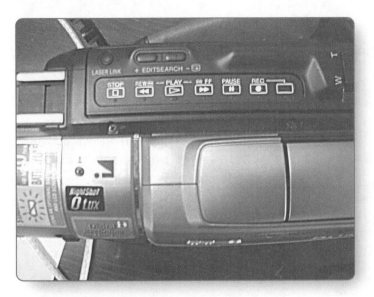

Set the VCR/TV selector to VCR. Press the Play button on your camcorder, and at the same time, press the Record button on your VCR. When you are finished copying the movie, press the Stop button on your VCR to stop recording.

Exporting Your Movie to QuickTime

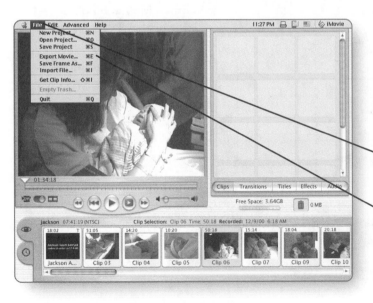

The QuickTime setting allows you to export your video into QuickTime's player, which compresses the iMovie file to ready it for e-mail, Web, or CD-ROM formats.

1. **Click** on **File**. The File menu will appear.

2. **Click** on **Export Movie**. The Export Movie dialog box will open.

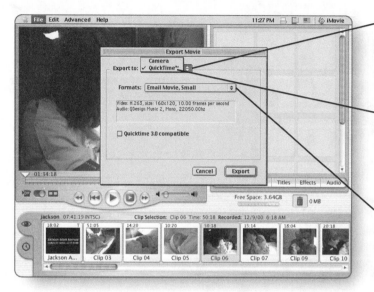

3. Click on the **up and down arrows** to the right of the Export to box. A pop-up menu will appear.

4. Click on **QuickTime**. The QuickTime settings will appear in the lower half of the dialog box.

5. Click on the **up and down arrows** to the right of the Formats box. A pop-up menu will appear.

6. Click on a **QuickTime movie format**. Your choices are the following:

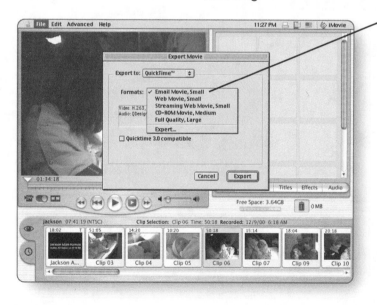

• **Email Movie, Small**. Select this option if you plan to send your movie as an e-mail attachment. Your iMovie is compressed into a relatively compact QuickTime movie.

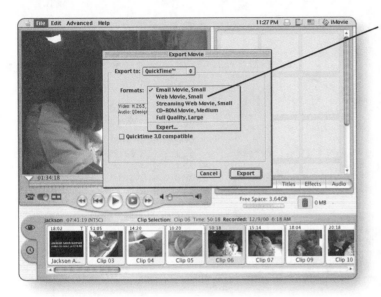

● **Web Movie, Small**. Select this option if you plan to post your movie on a Web page. The size of the QuickTime movie is bigger and the frame rate is higher than with the Email Movie, Small option and therefore provides better quality for the viewer. You still may want to use the Email Movie, Small option for posting on the Web because big movies may be difficult for people to download unless they have high-speed Internet connections. (Click on the QuickTime 3.0 compatible check box to create a movie that can be viewed by those who are still using QuickTime 3.0).

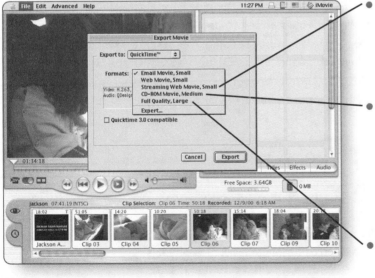

● **Streaming Web Movie, Small**. Select this option to prepare the movie for posting on a QuickTime streaming Web server.

● **CD-ROM Movie, Medium**. Select this option if you plan to record your movie onto a CD-ROM or if you plan to create a QuickTime movie to store and play on your hard drive.

● **Full Quality, Large**. You will probably never use this option. The file that this setting creates is massive. So, unless you're a pro, skip this option.

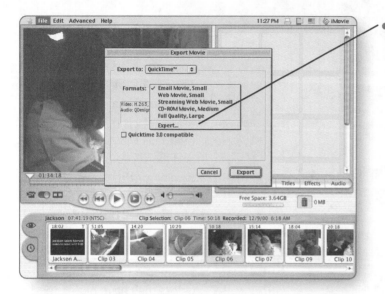

● **Expert**. The Expert settings are reserved for when you become a seasoned video compression guru. The iMovie creators have designed this software with all the compression settings the casual user should ever need, and therefore you should not have to change them. Using these settings goes beyond the scope of this book.

Notice that when you select a format, the video and audio compression specifications appear at the bottom of the Export Movie dialog box. This will give you an idea just how much your video needs to be compressed for these particular formats. For example, the video for a small QuickTime movie that you would attach to an e-mail message compresses from 30 to 10 frames per second. You definitely will lose a bit of playback quality in the QuickTime viewer, but it is necessary in order to compress your movie to a size that is viable for sending over the Internet or posting on a Web page.

NOTE

There are a few things to consider when choosing to send a QuickTime movie in an e-mail message. Even though iMovie compresses the file size, it is still a big file to send over the Internet as an e-mail attachment. For example, a 60-second movie will compress to approximately a 3 MB file, which is still fairly large. With that in mind, you need to make sure that the recipient of this file knows that you are sending it and can clear several minutes for the download.

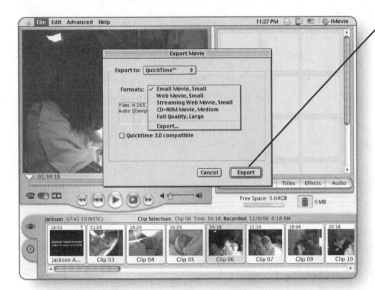

7. Click on the **Export button**. The Export QuickTime Movie dialog box will open.

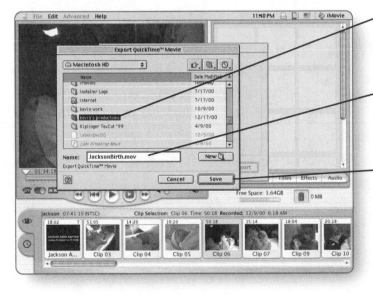

8. Click on the **folder** in which you want to save your movie. The folder will be selected.

9. Type a **title** for your QuickTime movie in the Name text box.

10. Click on **Save**. iMovie will begin to export your movie into a QuickTime file.

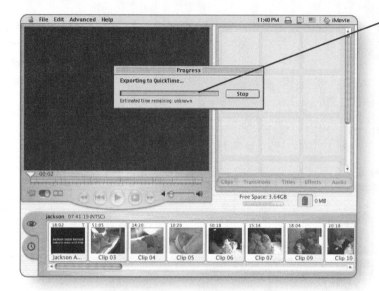

The Progress Bar will show your movie exporting to QuickTime. Depending on the size of your movie, this could take several minutes. So, leave the computer, grab a cannoli, and come back in a few minutes.

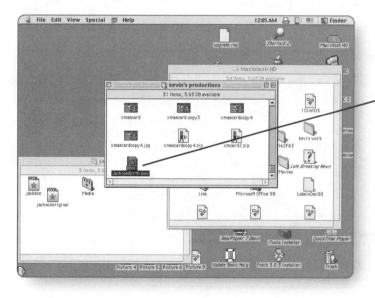

11. **Double-click** on the **folder** where you saved this QuickTime file. The folder will open.

12. **Double-click** on the **QuickTime movie file**. The QuickTime Player will open with your movie in it.

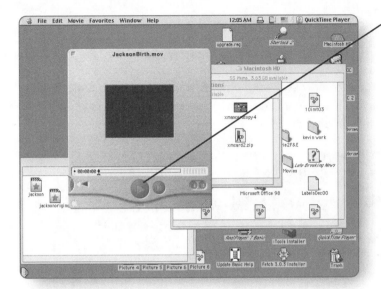

13. **Click** on the **Play button**.

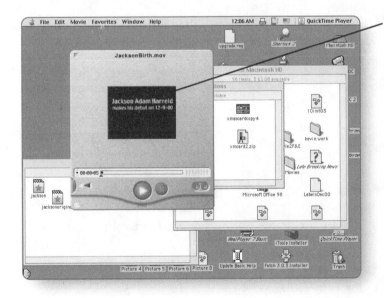

The QuickTime movie will play.

Understanding the QuickTime Player

iMovie compresses and exports your movies into QuickTime's Player. There you can play back your movie, adjust sound levels, and so on.

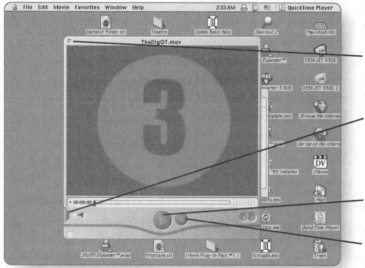

The QuickTime Player has the following features:

- **Close box**. Click on this box to close the QuickTime monitor window.

- **Volume wheel**. Press and hold the mouse button on this wheel and drag up or down to control volume.

- **Play button**. Click on this button to play the movie.

- **Pause/Stop button**. Click on this button to stop playback of the movie.

- **Resize handle**. Press and hold the mouse button on these slanted grooves and drag down and to the right to expand the Player, or up and to the left to shrink the Player.

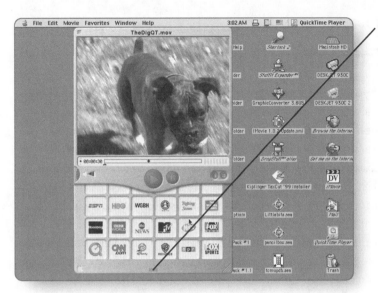

● **Favorites drawer**. Press and hold the mouse button on these horizontal grooves and drag down to reveal the Favorites panel. Here you can add icons of your movies.

● **Info button**. Click on this button to reveal any information about the movie that you are viewing. Click it again to hide the information. Usually only information (such as copyright info) from movies that you download from the Web will be housed here.

Importing QuickTime Clips into Your iMovies

If you have footage that is in a QuickTime movie file that you want to add to an iMovie, or you want to add footage of the wedding scene from the *Godfather* (in a QuickTime movie trailer) into your sister's wedding footage, iMovie and QuickTime Pro can handle the job. (This technique requires that you obtain the QuickTime Pro version, which is a $30 upgrade to your basic QuickTime version and is available at Apple's Web site.) Just remember the laws that govern redistribution of copyrighted material. Make sure that if you use that *Godfather* footage, you keep it for your own personal use. Otherwise, you'll sleep with the fishes.

1. Open the **QuickTime movie** that you want to insert into iMovie.

2. Click on **File**. The File menu will appear.

3. Click on **Export**. The Export dialog box will open.

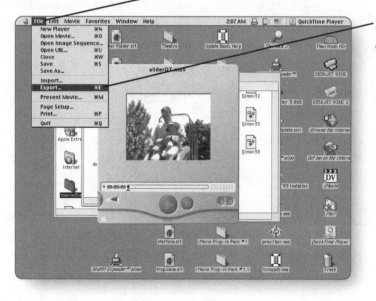

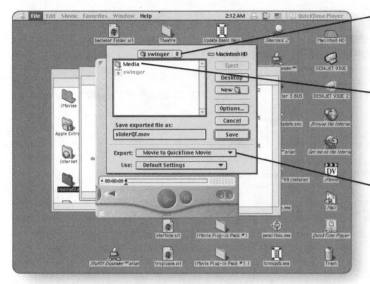

4. Click on the **folder** for the iMovie into which you want to add the QuickTime clip.

5. Click on the **Media folder** for the iMovie. This is where you will save the converted QuickTime clip.

6. Click on the **down arrow** to the right of the Export box. A drop-down list will appear.

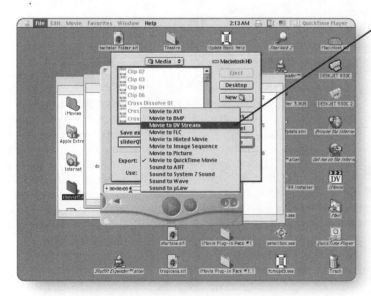

7. Click on **Movie to DV Stream**. The clip will change from a .mov file to a .dv file.

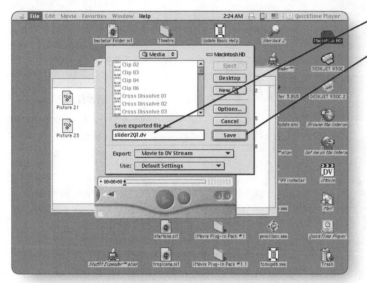

8. Type a **name** for your clip.

9. Click on **Save**. The clip will convert to a file that is compatible with your iMovie files.

10. Open iMovie.

11. Open the **iMovie project** that contains the QuickTime clip that you just exported.

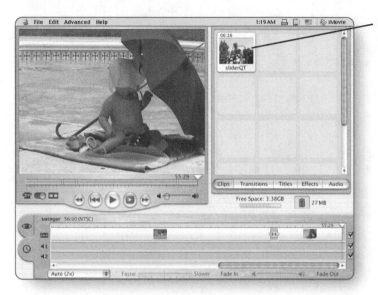

iMovie will load the clip onto the Scrolling Shelf for you.

Part III Review Questions

1. How do you establish the length of a transition? *See Setting Transition Speed in Chapter 6*

2. What is rendering? *See Adding the Transition in Chapter 6*

3. How can you add a title over a black background instead of over your video? *See Selecting a Title Background in Chapter 7*

4. Can you make a title align or scroll in a certain direction? See *Specifying Alignment and Scrolling Direction in Chapter 7*

5. How do you position a song to play precisely over a certain portion of your movie? *See Editing Audio Clips in Chapter 8*

6. How do you separate audio from a video clip? *See Extracting Audio from Video Clips in Chapter 8*

7. How can you add slow-motion effects to your clips? *See Creating Slow-Motion and Fast-Motion Effects in Chapter 9*

8. What kinds of special effects can you add to your movies? *See the introduction in Chapter 9*

9. Why would you want to make a copy of your iMovie? *See Making a Copy of Your iMovie in Chapter 10*

10. Why would you export your movie into a QuickTime file? *See Exporting Your Movie to QuickTime in Chapter 10*

iMovie 2 Extras

11

iMovie 2 and Still Images

Adding a still shot or series of still shots to your movie can add documentary-style impact. Another great feature of iMovie 2 is the capability to create a slide show or storyboard by using a series of still images, or to juxtapose stationary shots with your video clips to create an interesting montage of movement and still life. iMovie 2 allows you to import PICT, GIF, JPEG, BMP, and Photoshop files into your movies. It also allows you to create still images from your video footage to add to your movies or your collection of photographs taken with your traditional camera. You can even e-mail your still images to a friend or relative. In this chapter, you'll learn how to:

- Extract a still image from your video
- Create a still image in your movie
- Add a still image to your movie
- Set the frame rate or vary the duration of stills
- Add transitions, titles, and sound to slide shows

Extracting Still Images from Your Videos

There are many ways to obtain still images to import into your movies. If you have existing photographs, you can scan them and save them in PICT, GIF, JPEG, BMP, or Photoshop format. Or, you might already have stills on your hard drive in these formats. With iMovie, you can even create your own stills by pulling them from scenes in your videos.

1. **Click** on the **video clip** from which you want to extract the still image. The clip will appear in the Monitor window.

2. **Press and hold** the **mouse button** down on the playhead and **drag** the **playhead** left or right to locate the frame that you want to extract. The clip's footage will appear in the Monitor window as you drag.

TIP

To move one frame at a time, use the right and left arrow keys on your keyboard. This will make it easier for you to find the exact frame that you want.

---

3. **Release** the **mouse button**. The frame to extract will appear in the Monitor window.

4. **Click** on **File**. The File menu will appear.

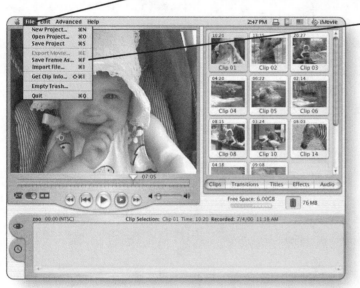

5. **Click** on **Save Frame As**. The Save Frame As Image dialog box will open.

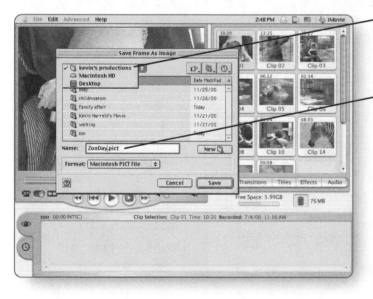

6. **Click** on a **folder** in which to save the image. The folder will be selected.

7. **Type** a **name** for the still image in the Name text box.

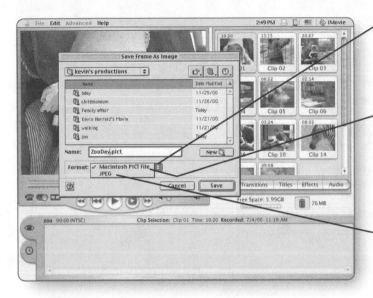

8. Click on the **up and down arrows** to the right of the Format list box. Two image format choices will appear.

9a. Click on **Macintosh PICT File** if you plan to use the still in an iMovie. The format will be selected.

OR

9b. Click on **JPEG** if you plan to use this image to e-mail to friends. The format will be selected.

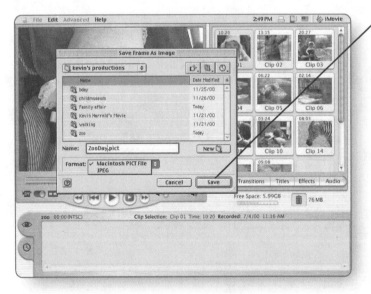

10. Click on **Save**. The image will be saved in the folder you designated.

NOTE

You might notice that your extracted stills sometimes have a grainy or jagged effect to them. iMovie will not produce the same high-quality digital stills as the new digital still cameras do. They should be good enough to include in movies and as e-mail attachments—they just might not be suitable for printing and framing.

Creating a Still Image within Your iMovie Project

In iMovie 2, you can create a still image from your footage while you are working on your video production. If you want to create a quick still to use as a background or as a stop-action effect in your movie, this is the technique to use. If you want to extract a still frame from your movie to save or print or send as an e-mail attachment, you should use the technique explained in "Extracting Still Images from Your Videos."

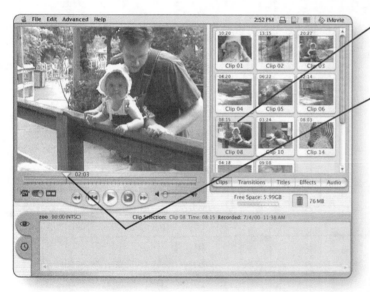

1. Click on the **clip** from which you want to create a still image. The clip will be selected.

2. Press and hold the **mouse button** down on the playhead and **drag it** to locate the frame from which you want to create a still image. The clip's footage will appear in the Monitor window as you drag. See the tip in the previous section regarding using the arrow keys for frame-by-frame playback.

3. Release the **mouse button**. The frame you want will appear in the Monitor window.

4. Click on **Edit**. The Edit menu will appear.

5. Click on **Create Still Clip**.

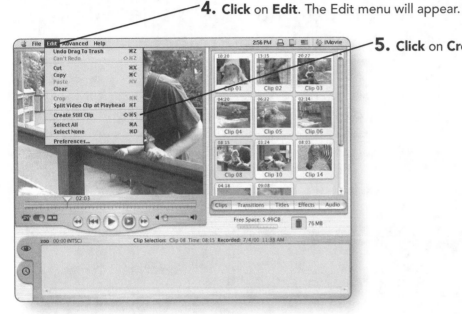

A still clip will be created. It will appear on the Scrolling Shelf with the name "Still *x*" (*x* being the sequential creation number of the still). You can add this still to your movie by dragging it down to the Clip Viewer.

Adding a Still Image to an iMovie

Inserting stills in your movies adds an interesting effect. Whether you want to create an entire "slide show" of stills or intersperse stills here and there within your video clips to create stop-action effects, you need to know how to import the stills into your iMovie project. If you have created a still from the project you're working on (as described in the previous section, "Creating a Still Image within Your iMovie Project"), then you're already in business; all you have to do is drag it from the Scrolling Shelf to the Clip Viewer to add it to your movie. If you want to use an image that currently exists outside your project, then you have to import that image into iMovie first.

1. **Click** on **File**. The File menu will appear.

2. **Click** on **Import File**. The Import File dialog box will open.

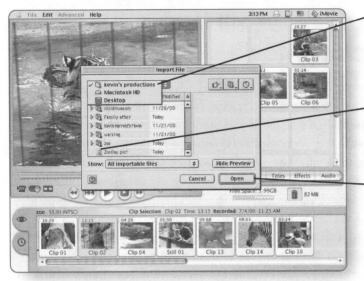

3. **Click** on the **folder** that contains the still image you want to import. The folder will open, revealing the images it contains.

4. **Click** on the **file name** of the still image you want to import. The image will be selected.

5. **Click** on **Open**.

The image will be imported to your project and will appear in the Scrolling Shelf and in the Monitor window.

6. **Press and hold** the **mouse button** on the still in the Scrolling Shelf and **drag it** to the Clip Viewer. The still will be added to your movie.

Setting or Varying the Duration of the Stills

You'll notice that iMovie 2 assigns a duration of 5 seconds (05:00) to still images. You can change this duration to be shorter in some stills or longer in others, or keep them all the same. You can also change that 5-second default duration so that every time you create or extract a still, your preferred duration is always automatically assigned. You're in charge, so there's no right or wrong way to do this. You might have a particularly striking image that you want on the screen for 5 seconds and another image that works better as a 1-second clip.

Changing the Duration of a Still Image

1. **Click** on a **still** whose duration you want to change. The still will be selected.

2. **Click** in the **Time box** in the Clip Viewer. The cursor will appear in the Time box.

TIP

iMovie assigns a default duration of 5 seconds to a still that you have imported. That can be an eternity in an iMovie. It's best to keep the duration at 2 to 3 seconds—just enough time for the audience to study the picture, but not enough time to bore them.

3. **Type** a **new duration** in the Time box.

4. **Press** the **Return key** on your keyboard. The new duration will take effect.

5. **Repeat steps 1 to 4** to set the duration for all of your stills.

Changing the Default Duration of Stills

1. **Click** on **Edit**. The Edit Menu will appear.

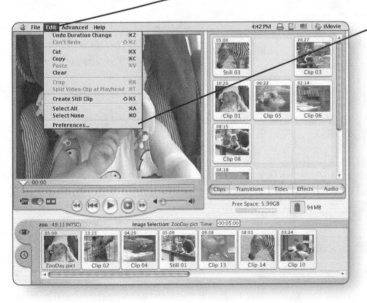

2. **Click** on **Preferences**. The Preferences dialog box will open.

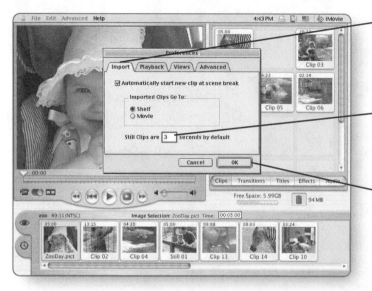

3. **Click** on the **Import tab**, if it isn't already selected. The Import tab will move to the front.

4. **Click** in the **Still Clips are … seconds by default text box** and **type** a new **duration**.

5. **Click** on **OK**. Your new default duration will take effect.

Creating a Slide Show

One of the coolest things you can do with still images in iMovie 2 is to create a slide show by using a series of stills. To produce a new slide show, open a new project.

1. **Click** on **File**. The File menu will appear.

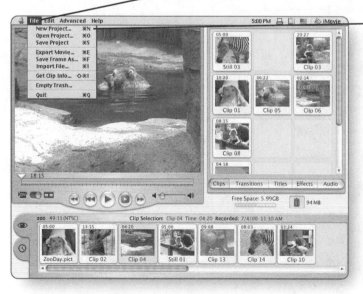

2. **Click** on **New Project**. The Create New Project dialog box will open.

3. Click on a **folder** in which to store your movie. The folder will be selected.

4. Type a **name** for your presentation in the Name field.

5. Click on **Create**. A new, blank canvas will appear for you to start your slide show.

Adding Stills to the Shelf and Timeline

Now that you have your blank canvas, you need to put something on it. Gather up your slides. If you already have them created or scanned in, you're ready to go. Otherwise, scan in your photos or extract a number of still images from your videos, as you learned earlier in the section "Extracting Still Images from Your Videos."

1. Click on **File**. The File menu will appear.

2. Click on **Import File**. The Import File dialog box will open.

3. Click on the **folder** where your still images are stored. The folder will open, revealing the images it contains.

4. Click on a **file** to select it. The file name will be highlighted.

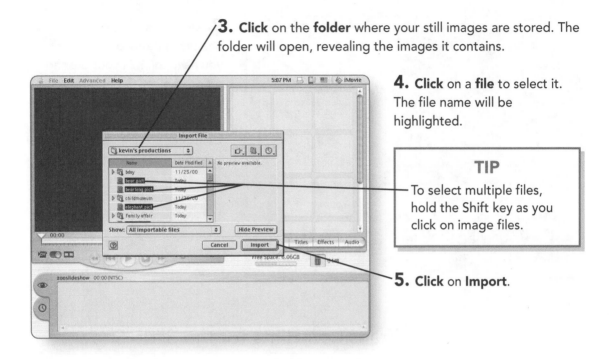

TIP

To select multiple files, hold the Shift key as you click on image files.

5. Click on **Import**.

The file or files will be imported to your project.

6. Repeat steps 1 through 5 until you have imported all of the slides you want into your project.

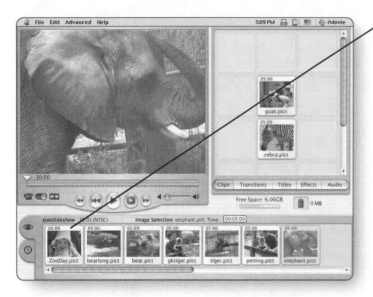

7. Drag and arrange your **images** in the Clip Viewer until you have them in your desired order, and **set** the **duration** of each still if you desire. A "movie" of still images will be created.

Transition Hints for the Slide Show

You can use any transition in your slide show, but I've found that the Push Right transition gives a project an authentic slide-show look. Refer to Chapter 6, "Adding Stylish Transitions," if you need a refresher on transition styles and how to use them.

1. Click on the **Transitions option** in the Design panel. The Transitions panel will appear.

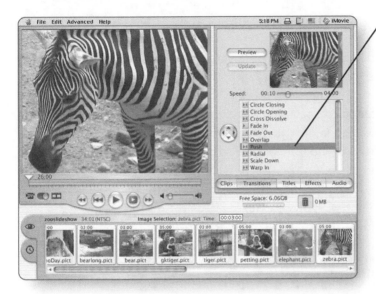

2. **Click** on a **transition type** in the Transitions panel. The transition will be selected.

3. **Click** on a **transition direction**. The direction will be set.

4. **Drag** the **duration slider** to your desired duration time for the transition. The new duration will be set.

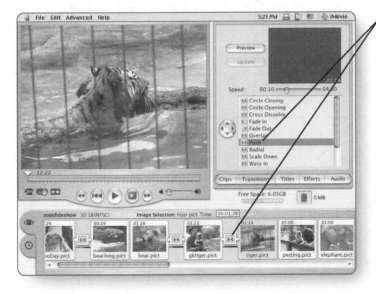

5. **Click and hold** the **mouse button** on the transition and **drag** the **transition** into place between your slides. The slides will move over a tad to make room for the transition.

6. **Release** the **mouse button**. The transition will appear and render between the slides.

7. **Repeat steps 1 through 6** to add all desired transitions to your slides.

Title Hints for the Slide Show

Adding small titles to individual slides is something that can be very effective for your slide show. For example, say you went on a family vacation, Clark W. Griswald–style, and wanted to document all of the different places you went and monuments you saw. You could add titles to your slides of the Grand Canyon, the largest ball of twine, Wally World, and so on.

Refer to Chapter 7, "Text in iMovie: Rolling Titles, Credits, and Captions," if you need to refresh yourself on any elements of creating and adding titles.

1. **Click** on the **Titles option** in the Design panel. The Titles panel will appear.

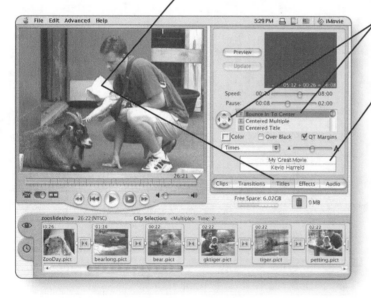

2. **Click** on a **title style and scrolling direction**. The style and direction will be selected.

3. **Type** your **title** in the title text box.

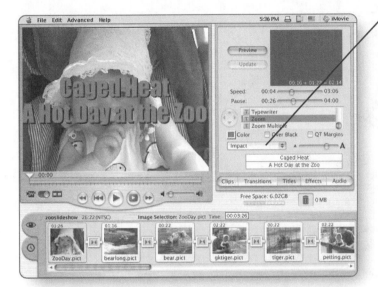

4. Click on a **font style**. The font will be selected.

5. Click on a **font color**. The font color will be selected.

6. Drag the **Speed and Pause sliders** to your desired settings. The durations will be set.

7. **Drag** your **finished title** to the desired still in the Clip Viewer.

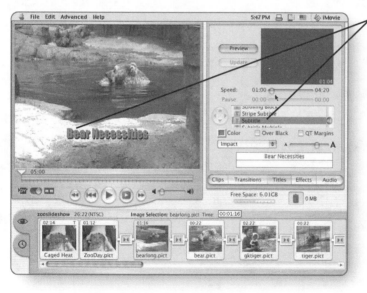

8. **Add** any other **small titles** to your slides, such as dates or quotes. The Subtitle style works great for this type of effect.

Sound Advice for Your Slide Show

Because there won't be any sound with your stills, it's almost necessary to add some kind of soundtrack or narration to your slide show. Think of the mood that you want your project to have and add a melody to set the tone of the slide show. Take another look at Chapter 8, "Audio: Adding Soundtracks, Scores, Sounds, and Narration," if you need to review how to do anything in this section.

1. Insert the **CD** that has the song you want or **import** an **audio file** from your hard drive.

2. Click on **Audio** in the Design panel. The Audio panel will appear.

3. Click on the **Timeline Viewer tab**. The Timeline Viewer will appear.

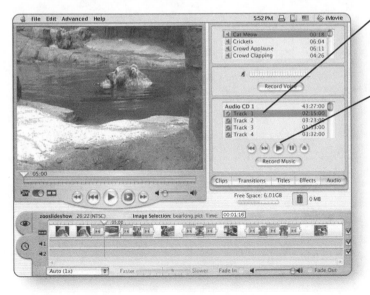

4. Click on the **track** you want to use. The track will be selected.

5. Click on the **Play button**. The audio track will play. Make sure the playhead is located where you want your music to begin recording.

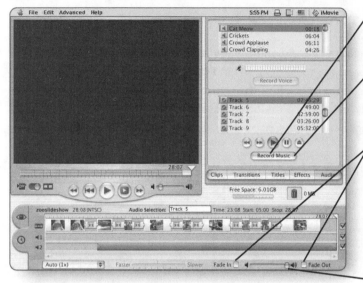

6. **Click** on **Record Music**. The music will start recording.

7. **Click** on **Stop Recording** when you want the recording to cease.

8. **Click** on the **Fade In and Fade Out check boxes** in the Audio Viewer to fade your music in and out at the beginning and end of your slide show.

9. **Drag** the **sound slider** to adjust the volume on your recording.

12

Tricks with Text

Are you not getting the text effects you desire from the titles in iMovie 2? You can give the text in your titles and credits more pizzazz by taking advantage of other photo manipulation and paint programs outside of iMovie 2 and importing the finished files into iMovie. Photoshop, PhotoDeluxe, and even AppleWorks's paint program allow you to go a few steps further with text, images, patterns, gradients, filters, and so on. Take the ideas used in this chapter and adapt them to fit your needs in your own movies. In this chapter, you'll learn how to:

- Create opening film countdowns
- Add more exciting titles
- Insert silent-film dialog placards
- Add silent-film sound effects

Creating an Opening Film Countdown

I like the look and feel of silent films and film noir. Remember the old films that had the numbers counting down before the film began? Duplicating an effect like this and the others you'll create in this chapter can help give your movie a *Touch of Evil*. Begin by opening whatever photo manipulation or paint program you have. I use Photoshop 4.0 in this chapter, but the techniques I show you should be similar in other programs, and I'll point out differences here and there.

Preparing Your Canvas

Before you create the number sequence, you need to ready your canvas. This canvas will be used as the starting point for all of your numbers in this effect.

1. Open your **photo manipulation or paint program**.

2. Click on **File**. The File menu will appear.

3. Click on **New**. The New dialog box will open.

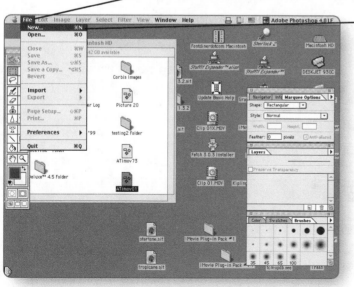

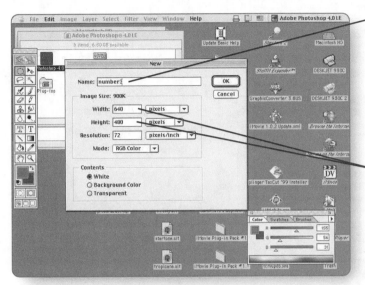

4. **Type** a **new name** for the file.

5. **Set** all the **margins** to 0, if your program asks you to. Some programs will not ask you for this option.

6. **Set** the **size** of the image (width and height) to 640 pixels by 480 pixels. The size will be set.

NOTE

640 by 480 pixels is the size of the frame that will fit in iMovie without any cropping or additions of a border, so it is important to make this the dimension of your images.

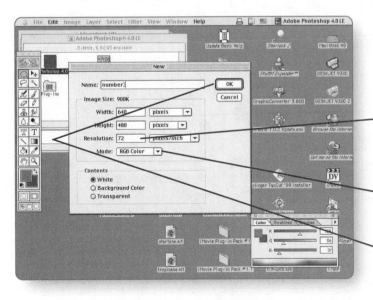

7. **Set** the **resolution** to 72 pixels/inch. The resolution will be set.

8. **Set** the **mode** to RGB Color. The mode will be set.

9. **Click** on **OK**. A blank canvas will appear.

Creating the First Number

Now that you have the canvas prepared, you're ready to create the first number in your countdown sequence.

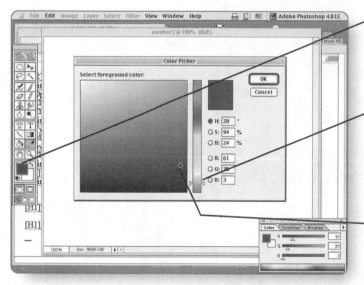

1. **Click** on the **foreground color box**. The color selector or Color Picker dialog box will open.

2. **Click** on a **color range** on the vertical color bar to select the overall color for your canvas. The color range you selected will appear.

3. **Move** the **mouse pointer** to the large box to the left of the vertical color bar. The mouse pointer will change to a circle.

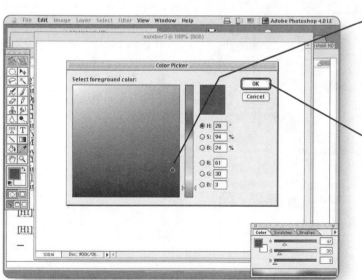

4. **Click** on a **color**. Select a color that has some black tones in it, because you want this effect to have an older, slightly black-and-white look.

5. **Click** on **OK**. The color will be selected.

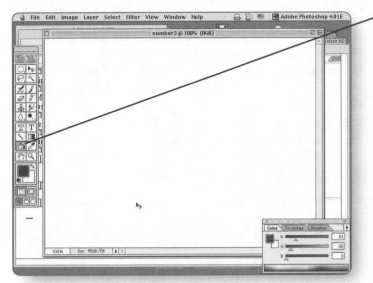

6. Click on the **Fill or Paint Bucket tool**. The tool will be selected, and the mouse pointer will change to a paint bucket icon.

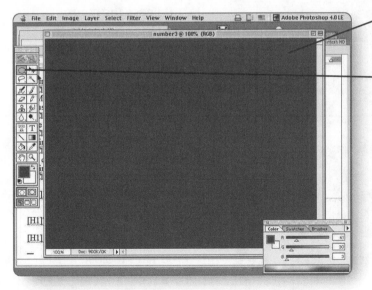

7. Click on the **canvas**. The color will fill up the canvas.

8. Click on the **Oval Marquee tool**. The tool will be selected, and the mouse pointer will change to a crosshair.

NOTE

If the toolbox is showing a dotted-line rectangle, or Rectangular Marquee tool, you have to change it to the dotted-line circle, or Oval Marquee tool. Just press and hold the mouse button on the Rectangular Marquee tool until a pop-up menu appears. Then, move the mouse pointer over to the dotted-line oval icon and release the mouse button. The tool will change to the Oval Marquee tool.

9. **Press and hold** the **mouse button** near the upper-left corner of your canvas and **drag** the **mouse** to the lower-right corner of the canvas to form a circle. A dotted-line circle will appear as you drag.

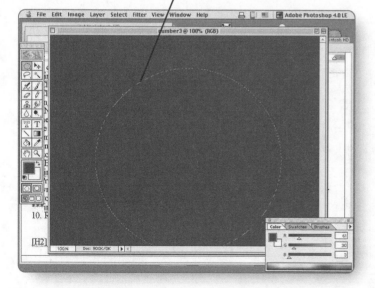

10. **Release** the **mouse button**. The circle will appear, and your mouse pointer will change to a Move tool.

NOTE

Depending on the program you are using, the mouse pointer may or may not automatically change to a Move tool. If it doesn't, just select the Move tool from your program's toolbar. Most programs' Move tools will look like an arrow icon.

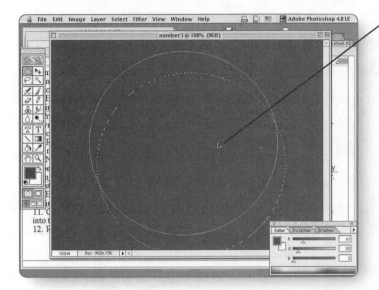

11. **Click and hold** the **mouse button** in the circle you just created and **drag** the **circle** into the center of the canvas.

12. **Release** the **mouse button**. The circle will now be located in the center of the canvas.

13. **Click** on the **foreground color square** again. The Color Picker will open.

14. **Click** on a **color** that is just a shade lighter than the color you selected for your background. The color will be selected.

15. **Click** on **OK**. The new color will be selected.

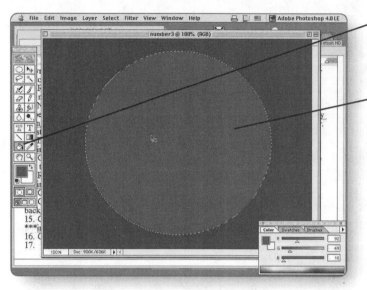

16. Click on the **Fill or Paint Bucket tool**. The tool will be selected.

17. Click inside the **circle** you made. The circle will be filled with your new color.

18. Click on the **foreground color square** again. The Color Picker will open.

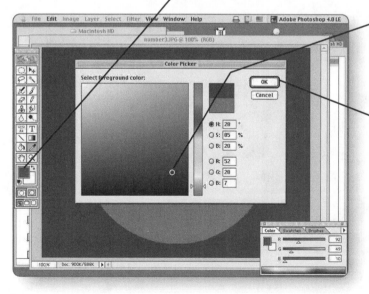

19. Select a **slightly darker shade** of the previous color tone you selected. The color will be selected.

20. Click on **OK**. The Color Picker will close.

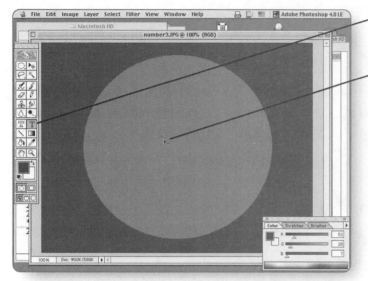

21. **Click** on the **Type tool**. The Type tool will be selected.

22. **Click** in the **center** of the circle. The Type Tool dialog box will open.

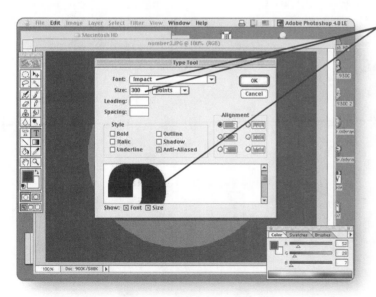

23. **Select** a **font style and size** and **type 3** in the text box that appears at the bottom of the dialog box.

24. **Click** on **OK**. The number 3 will appear on your canvas.

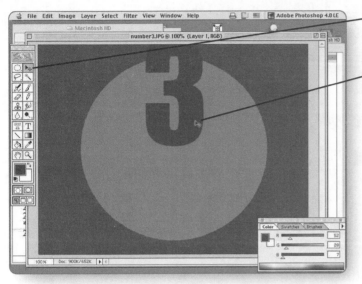

25. Click on the **Move tool**. The Move tool will be selected.

26. Press and hold the **mouse button** on the number 3 and drag the **number** to center it in your circle.

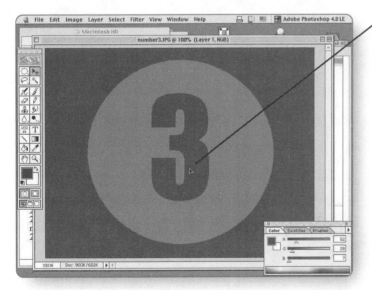

27. Release the **mouse button**. The number will be centered.

28. Click on **File**. The File menu will appear.

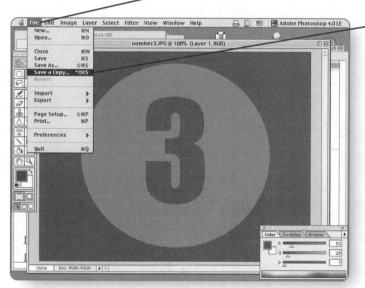

29. Click on **Save a Copy**. The Save dialog box will open.

> ### NOTE
> You want to save a copy of the file because you will be using this file again to make more numbers.

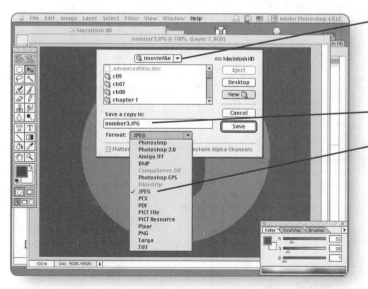

30. Click on the **down arrow** to select a folder in which to save your file. The folder will be selected.

31. Type a **name** for your file.

32. Click on **JPEG** in the Format drop-down list to use as your file format. A check mark will appear next to JPEG.

You have finished your first number image. Make sure you keep this file open, because in the next section you will use this to create the other number images for your countdown effect.

Creating the Other Numbers

Depending on the image program you are using, you can easily convert the file you created in the previous section into your other number images. Photoshop, for example, uses a process called *layers*, in which each different element you create in a single file becomes a separate layer that you can manipulate, move, edit, and so on. If your program doesn't use layers, you can just start over and repeat the previous section's steps. This section describes how to use the layers process.

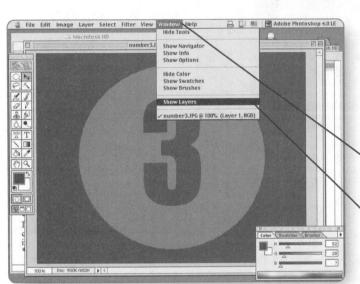

1. Click on **Window**. The Window menu will appear.

2. Click on **Show Layers**. The Layers window will open.

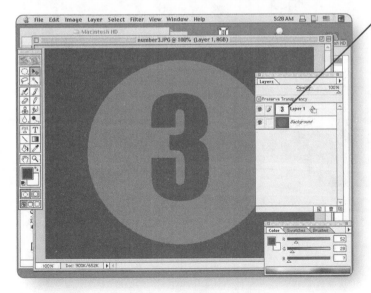

3. Press and hold the **mouse button** down on the layer containing the number 3 and **drag it** to the trash can.

4. Release the **mouse button**. The 3 will disappear from your canvas, and you will be left with just the background and circle.

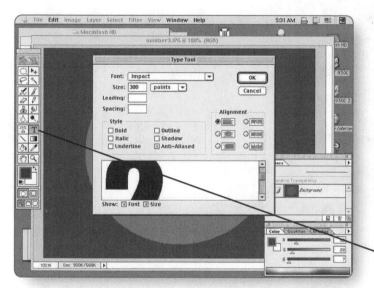

5. Click on the **Type tool**. The Type tool will be selected.

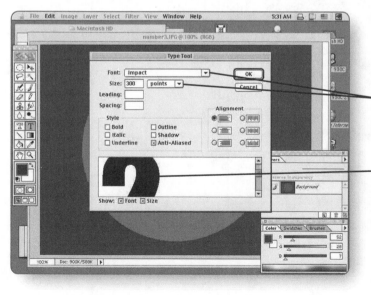

6. Click in the **center** of the circle. The Type Tool dialog box will open.

7. Select the **same font style and size** as you did for the first number.

8. Type 2 in the text box.

9. Click on **OK**. The number 2 will appear on your canvas.

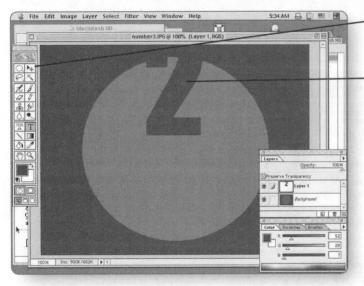

10. **Click** the **Move tool**. The Move tool will be selected.

11. **Press and hold** the **mouse button** on the number 2 and **drag it** to the center of the circle.

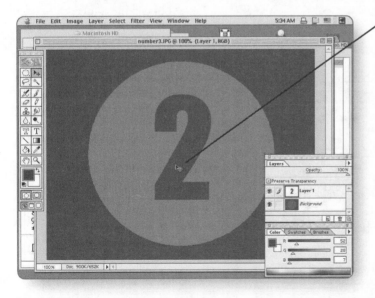

12. **Release** the **mouse button**. The number 2 will be centered.

13. Click on **File**. The File menu will appear.

14. Click on **Save a Copy**. The Save dialog box will open.

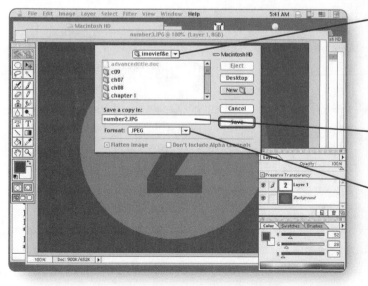

15. Click on the **down arrow** to select a folder in which to save your number 2. Save it in the same folder as your number 3.

16. Type a **name** for your number 2 file.

17. Click on **JPEG** from the Format drop-down list. JPEG will be selected.

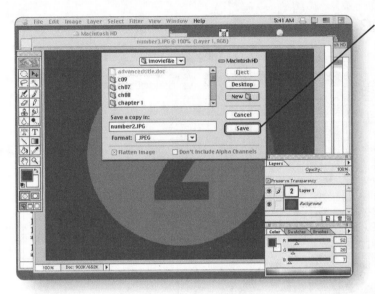

18. Click on **Save**. Your number 2 will be saved.

19. Repeat steps 3 through 12 to create a number 1.

NOTE

The Layers window should still be open, unless you closed it. If it is not open, click on Window and then click on Show Layers.

Adding the Images to Your Movie

Now that you've created your images, you need to add them to your iMovie production.

1. Open iMovie.

2. Open the **iMovie project** into which you want to import your newly created files.

3. **Click** on **File**. The File menu will appear.

4. **Click** on **Import File**. The Import File dialog box will open.

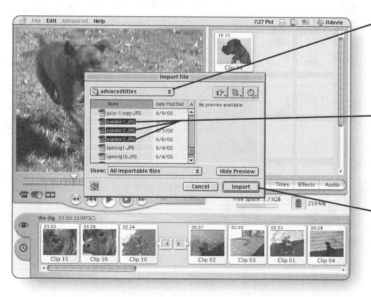

5. **Click** on the **folder** in which your countdown-number images reside. The folder will open and reveal your image files.

6. **Press** the **Shift key** and **click** on the three **images** that you created. The images will be selected.

7. **Click** on **Import**. The files will be imported to the Shelf in your iMovie project.

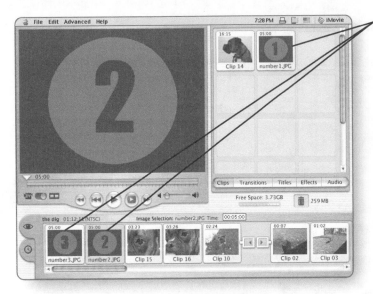

8. Drag the **images** from the Shelf and drop them in the Clip Viewer. The clips will appear in the Clip Viewer.

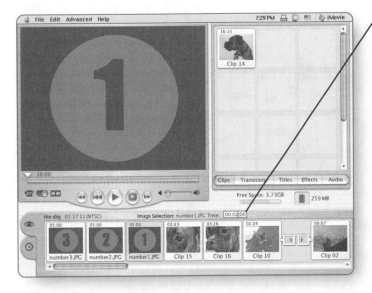

9. Click in the **duration box** and **type** a **duration** for each clip; approximately 2 seconds works well.

10. Press the **Enter key**. The new duration will be set.

Adding Transitions

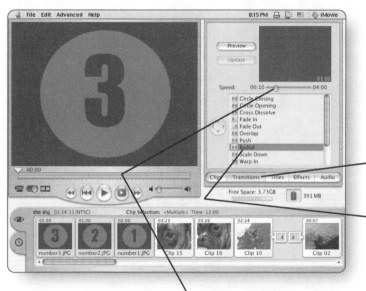

If you want, add a transition between the images you just created. You can get that old, numbered-countdown effect without any transition, but it looks even better with the Radial transition.

1. Click on **Transitions**. The Transitions panel will open.

2. Click on **Radial**. The Radial transition will be selected.

3. Drag the **duration slider** to about 1:20. The transition duration will be set.

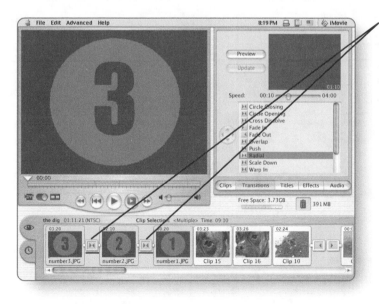

4. Drag and drop the **transition** between the images of the 3 and the 2 and between the 2 and the 1. The transitions will appear between the numbers and begin to render.

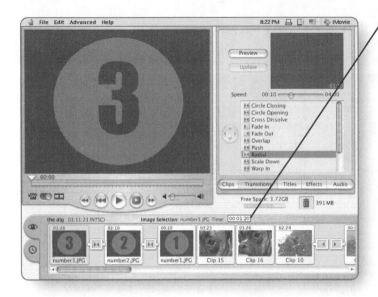

5. **Select** each of your **number clips** and **change** the **duration time** to equal lengths in the duration text box if you want to change the duration of the clips.

Playing Your Effect

To see if everything is the way you want it, you can play back just those clips you worked on and then make any desired changes.

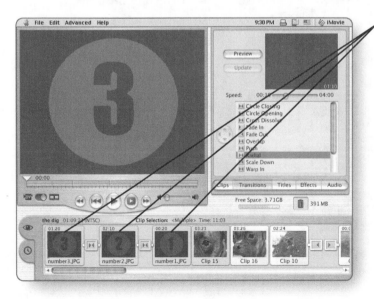

1. **Press** the **Shift button** and **click** on all the **clips** you want to play back. The clips, and the transitions between them, will be selected.

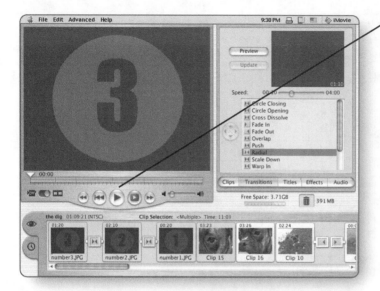

2. Click on the **Play button** in the Monitor window. The selected clips will play back in the Monitor window.

3. Make any desired **adjustments** to the effect you created.

Controlling the Look of Your Titles

Using another program, you can harness more control over your titles in iMovie 2. You have more freedom with text size, position, color, and style using programs other than iMovie to create titles. Let's add a title that complements the numbered-countdown effects you created in the previous section.

Preparing Your Canvas

You again need to ready your canvas for your title in the same manner as you did with the number sequence.

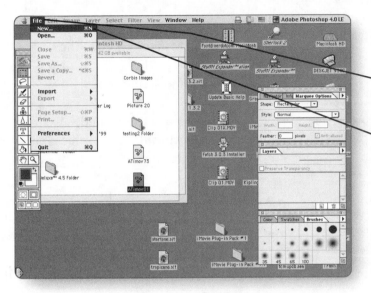

1. Open your **image manipulation program**.

2. Click on **File**. The File menu will appear.

3. Click on **New**. The New dialog box will open.

4. Type a **new name** for the file.

5. Set all **margins** to 0, if your program asks you to. The margins will be set.

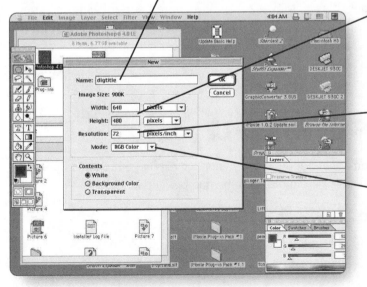

6. Set the **dimensions** for the image size (width and height) to 640 by 480 pixels. The dimensions will be set.

7. Set the **resolution** to 72 pixels/inch. The resolution will be set.

8. Set the **mode** to RGB Color. The mode will be set.

9. Click on **OK**. Your blank canvas will appear.

Creating the Title

Now start creating your title. Remember, you want it to have a similar look to your number sequence.

1. Click on the **foreground color square**. The color selector or Color Picker will open.

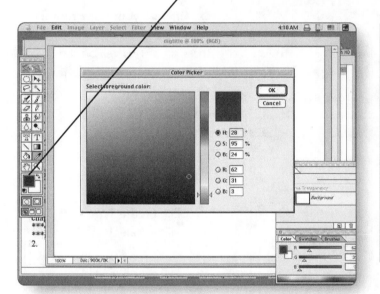

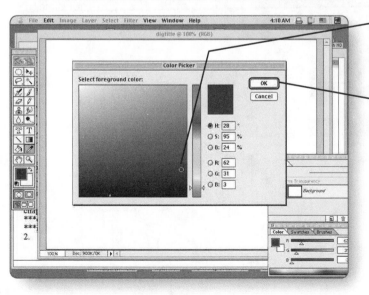

2. Choose a **color** in the Color Picker. The color will be selected.

3. Click on **OK**. The Color Picker dialog box will close, and you will be returned to your canvas.

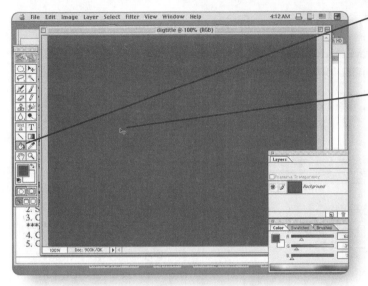

4. Click on the **Fill or Paint Bucket tool**. The tool will be selected.

5. Click on your **canvas**. The color will fill the canvas.

6. Change your **foreground color** like you did in steps 1 through 3. This will be the color of your text, so you might want to match it with the text used in the numbered-countdown effect.

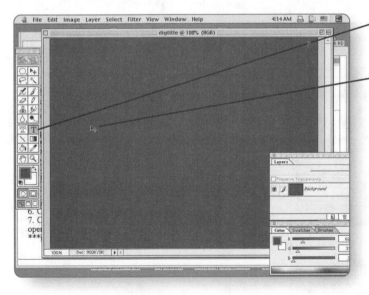

7. Click on the **Type tool**. The tool will be selected.

8. Click on the **canvas** approximately where you want the title. The Type Tool dialog box will open.

9. Set the **font style and size**. You should keep the same font settings as those you used in the numbered-countdown effect.

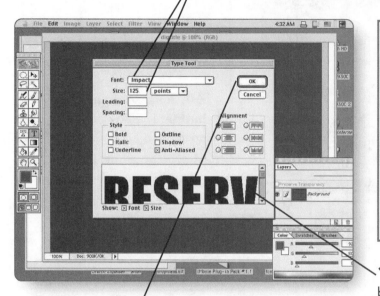

TIP

For titles, remember that it is always best to use thicker, bolder fonts because they will eventually appear on televisions, QuickTime videos, and so on. Thinner fonts and script-type fonts tend to be difficult to read in those formats.

10. Type your **title** in the text box.

11. Click on **OK**. Your title will appear on your canvas.

NOTE

If you want several stacked lines or a block of text hovering over your movie title—as in, "A Film by *So and So*"—repeat steps 7 through 11 and adjust the text accordingly. You might want to use different colors or font sizes for these other text elements in order to create a nice effect. You also have the freedom to move these different text elements around the page separate from the other text elements. Or, if you don't want the title of your movie on the same page as your block of text, you can always create completely separate images and insert them among your video clips for an equally interesting title scheme.

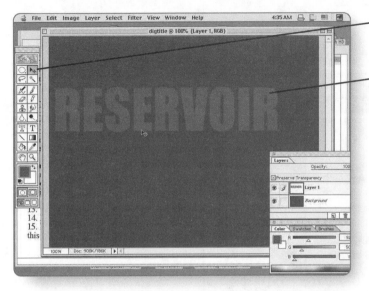

12. **Click** on the **Move tool**. The Move tool will be selected.

13. **Click and hold** the **mouse button** on the title and **drag** the **title** to your desired location.

14. **Release** the **mouse button**. The title will be in position.

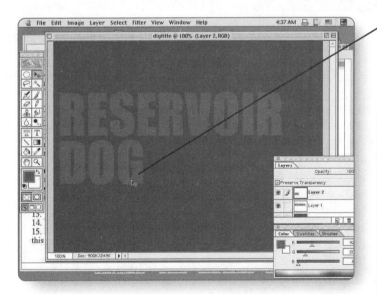

15. **Repeat steps 7 through 14** for any other part of your title or any other text you want to insert on this page.

NOTE

In many image programs, you can add interesting effects to your text, such as drop shadows, beveling and embossing, and so on. Feel free to take advantage of these effects. See your program's help files to learn how to utilize these effects.

16. **Click** on **File**. The File menu will appear.

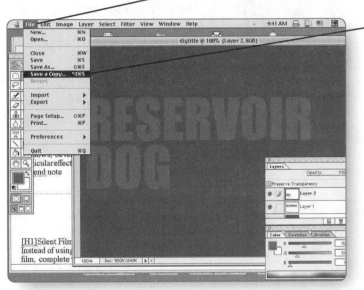

17. **Click** on **Save a Copy**. The Save dialog box will open.

18. **Click** on a **folder** in which to save the title image. The folder will open.

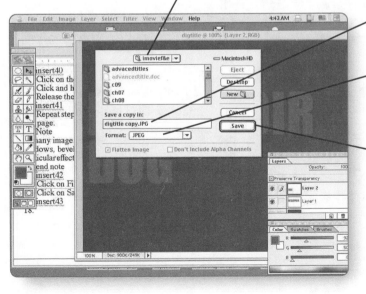

19. **Type** a **name** for the image.

20. **Click** on **JPEG** in the Format drop-down list. JPEG will be selected.

21. **Click** on **Save**. The image will be saved.

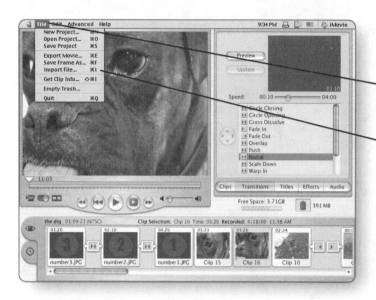

22. **Open** your **iMovie project**. The project will open.

23. **Click** on **File**. The File menu will appear.

24. **Click** on **Import File**. The Import File dialog box will open.

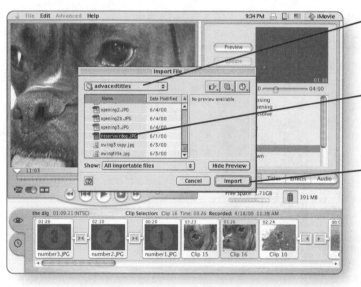

25. **Click** on the **folder** in which your title image is saved. The folder will open.

26. **Click** on the **title image** you just created. The image will be selected.

27. **Click** on **Import**. The image will be imported to the iMovie Shelf.

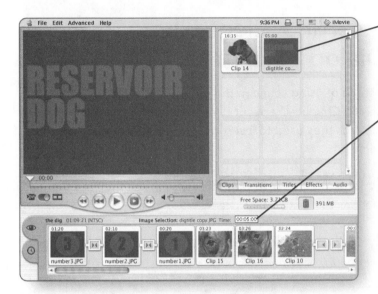

28. **Drag** the **image** from the Shelf and drop it on the Clip Viewer. The image will appear in the Clip Viewer.

29. **Set** the **duration** of your title. The duration will be set.

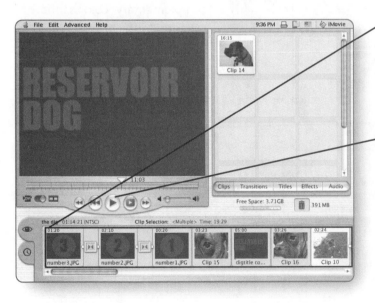

30. **Press** the **Shift key** and **click** on a **group of clips** that surround the title and countdown effects. The clips will be selected.

31. **Click** on the **Play button** in the Monitor window. The selected clips will play.

Inserting Silent-Film Dialog Placards

Instead of using sound in this movie, let's try making this a Charlie Chaplin–like silent film, complete with those dialog placards they used to insert between the moving picture frames.

1. **Repeat steps 1 through 9** in the "Preparing Your Canvas" sections to create a blank canvas.

2. Click on the **foreground color square**. The Color Picker will open.

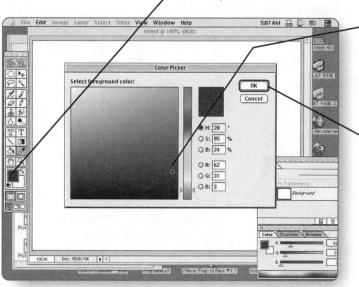

3. Click on a **color**. Remember to select the same (or a complementary) color as the other text effects you created in this chapter.

4. Click on **OK**. The color will be selected.

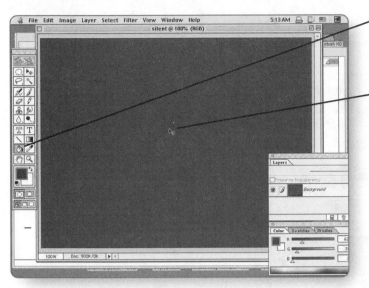

5. Click on the **Fill or Paint Bucket tool**. The tool will be selected.

6. Click on the **canvas**. The color will fill the canvas.

7. Click on the **foreground color square** again. The Color Picker will open.

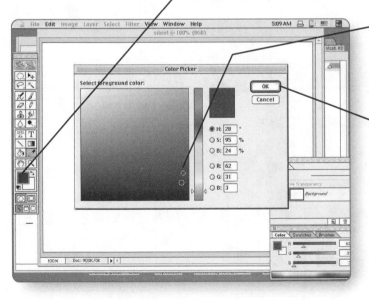

8. Select the **same color** as the text you used in the previous text effects sections of this chapter.

9. Click on **OK**. The color will be selected.

10. **Click** on the **Marquee or Rectangular selection tool**. The Marquee tool's options palette will open.

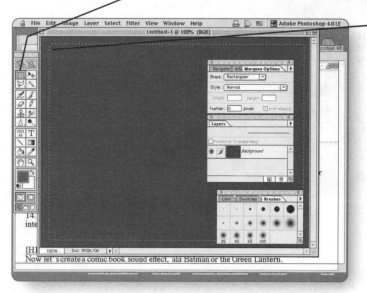

11. **Click and hold** the **mouse pointer** in the upper-left corner of your canvas and **drag** the **mouse** down to the lower-right corner of your canvas to form a rectangle just inside the outer edge of your canvas.

12. **Release** the **mouse button**. A marching-ants square will appear.

13. **Click** on **Select**. The Select menu will appear.

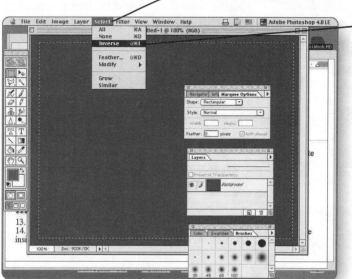

14. **Click** on **Inverse**. The area outside of the marching ants will be selected, instead of the inside.

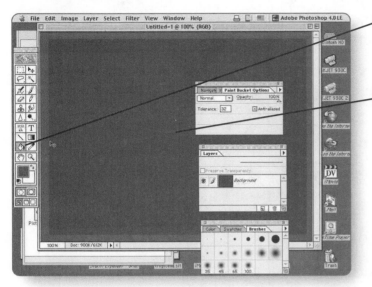

15. **Click** on the **Paint Bucket or Fill tool**. The tool will be selected.

16. **Click** in your **canvas**. The border will be filled with the color.

17. **Click** on **File**. The File menu will appear.

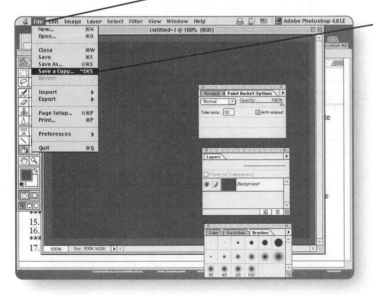

18. **Click** on **Save a Copy**. The Save dialog box will open. You want to save a copy of this image because you are going to reuse it with different sets of dialog throughout your movie.

19. **Click** on a **folder** in which to save your image. The folder will be selected.

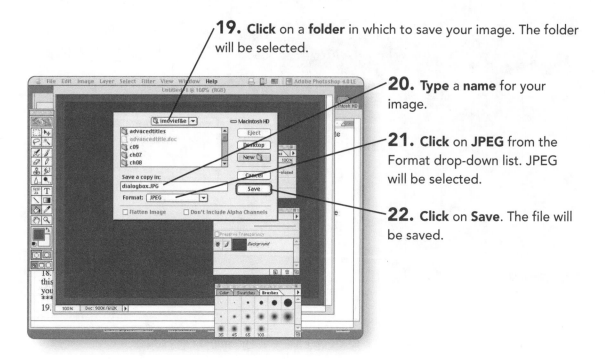

20. **Type** a **name** for your image.

21. **Click** on **JPEG** from the Format drop-down list. JPEG will be selected.

22. **Click** on **Save**. The file will be saved.

23. **Click** on the **Type tool**. The Type tool will be selected.

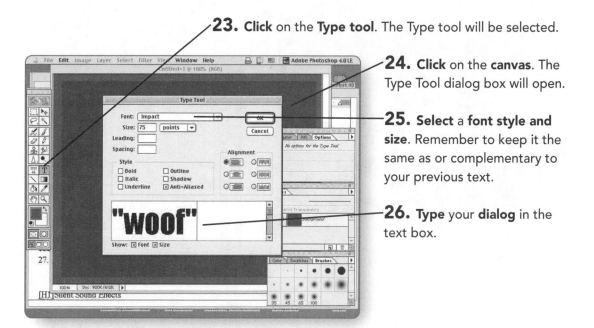

24. **Click** on the **canvas**. The Type Tool dialog box will open.

25. **Select** a **font style and size**. Remember to keep it the same as or complementary to your previous text.

26. **Type** your **dialog** in the text box.

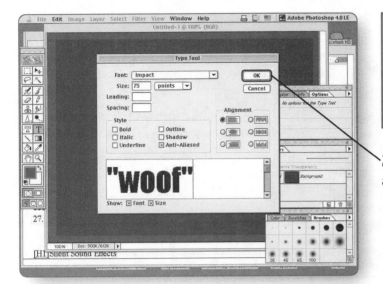

27. **Click** on **OK**. The text will appear in your canvas.

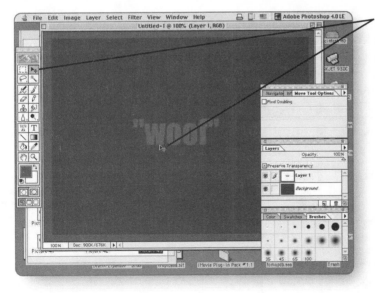

28. **Click** on the **Move tool** and **center** your **text**. The text will be centered.

29. **Click** on **File**. The File menu will appear.

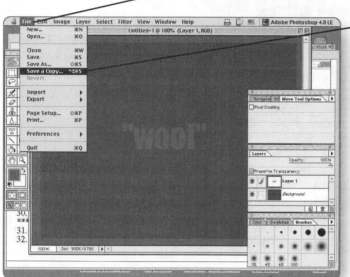

30. **Click** on **Save a Copy**. The file will be saved.

31. **Repeat** this **process** to create other silent dialog placards.

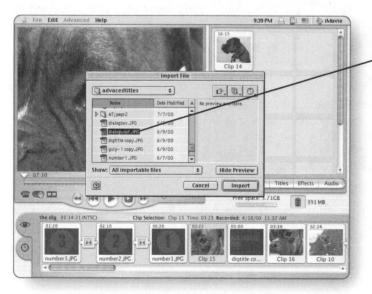

32. **Open iMovie**.

33. **Import** the **files** you created. The files will be imported.

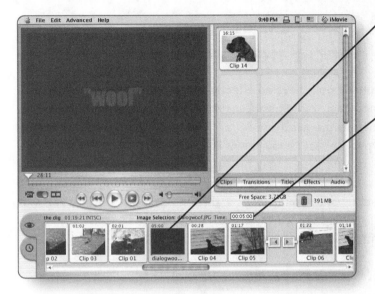

34. **Move** the **images** into place in your movie. The images will be positioned where you want them.

35. **Adjust** the **duration** of your dialog clips. The new durations will be set.

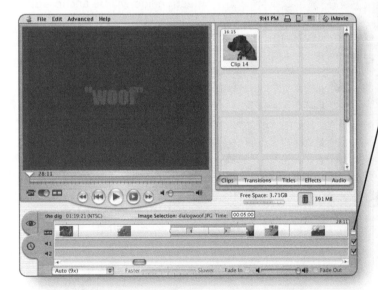

TIP

To have a true silent film, you should turn off the audio in the audio track, which you learned how to do in Chapter 8, "Audio: Adding Soundtracks, Scores, Sounds, and Narration." Click on the Timeline tab and then click to remove the check mark at the right end of the audio track bar. Also, adding a soundtrack to silent films is very effective. Try using that crazy, rapid-pace music from old Charlie Chaplain or Buster Keaton films.

Adding Silent-Film Sound Effects

Comic books have an effective way to tell the reader that an important sound has occurred. An entire storyboard frame encases the word "Pow!" or "Crash!" You can create the same type of effect in your silent iMovie.

1. Repeat all the **steps** in the "Preparing Your Canvas" section and **repeat steps 2 through 6** of the previous section ("Inserting Silent-Film Dialog Placards") to fill your canvas with color.

2. Click on the **Polygon Lasso tool**. The tool will be selected.

3. Click on the **canvas**. The selection line will be anchored.

4. Move the **mouse pointer** to draw a line and **click again** to end the line. Continue in this fashion until you have a starburst-type shape.

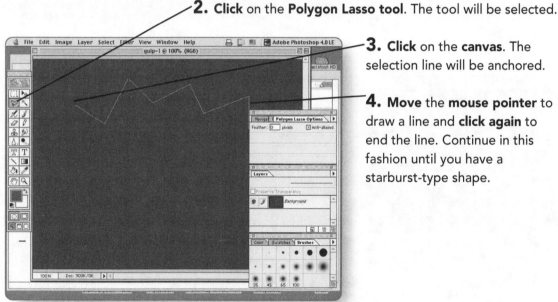

5. Connect the **final line** with the starting line. The selection will be complete and marching ants will appear to indicate your selection.

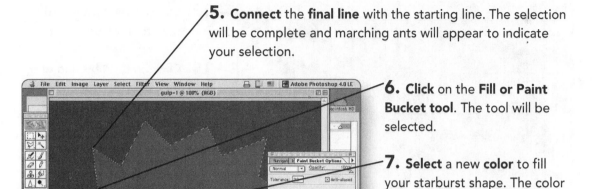

6. Click on the **Fill or Paint Bucket tool**. The tool will be selected.

7. Select a new **color** to fill your starburst shape. The color will be selected.

8. Click in the **starburst**. The starburst will fill with the new color.

9. Click on the **Type tool**. The tool will be selected.

10. Click in the **starburst**. The Type Tool dialog box will open.

11. Select your **font style and size** and **type** your **text**.

12. Click on **OK**. The text will appear in the starburst.

13. Click on the **Move tool**. The Move tool will be selected.

14. Click on the **text** and **drag it** to the center of your canvas. The text will move into place.

15. Click on **Layer**. The Layer menu will appear.

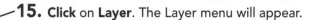

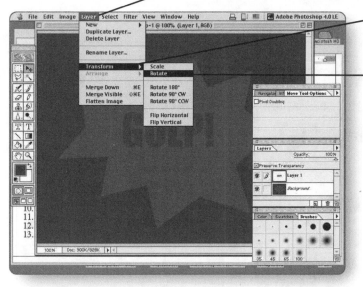

16. Click on **Transform**. The Transform submenu will appear.

17. Click on **Rotate**. Sizing handles will appear around your text.

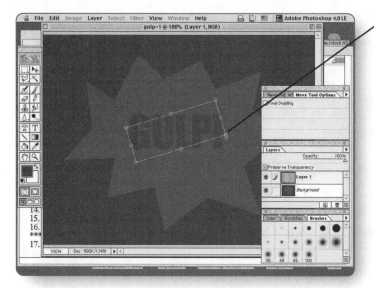

18. **Press and hold** the **mouse button** on one of the sizing handles and **drag** the **handle** up or down. The text will rotate up or down.

19. **Release** the **mouse button**. The text will appear rotated in the starburst.

20. **Click** on **Save a Copy**. Your file will be saved.

21. **Repeat** this **process** to create other silent-film sound effect images.

22. Open iMovie and **import** the **files** you created. The files will be imported into your iMovie project.

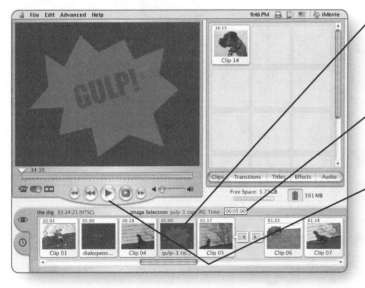

23. Drag and drop the **files** into place in the Clip Viewer. The files will appear in the Clip Viewer.

24. Adjust the **duration** of your clips. The new durations will be set.

25. Select all of your clips and view your entire silent-film masterpiece!

13

Getting Your Movie on the Web

A great way to premiere your movie is to post it on a Web site. This way, family and friends can go to your Web site and view your movie at their leisure. You don't clog their e-mail with a huge attachment, and you don't spend time and money on videotapes and postage sending Junior's home run to everyone. Apple provides a nifty service especially for iMovie makers: you can create your own Web site and add a page to it that showcases your iMovies. In this chapter, you'll learn how to:

- Set up an iTools account
- Access your iDisk
- Create and edit your home page
- Add your movie to your home page

Setting Up an iTools Account

The first step in creating a Web page to showcase your iMovies is to sign up for and open an Apple iTools account. iTools is a free Internet service provided by Apple for Macintosh users. It allows you to create an e-mail address, make the Internet safer for your kids, store files on Apple's Internet server, and create your own personal Web site.

1. Go to **Apple's Web site** (http://www.apple.com). The Apple home page will appear.

2. Click on the **iTools tab**. The iTools page will appear.

3. Scroll down the **page** and **read** what you can do with iTools.

4. Click on **Free Sign Up**. The iTools setup page will appear.

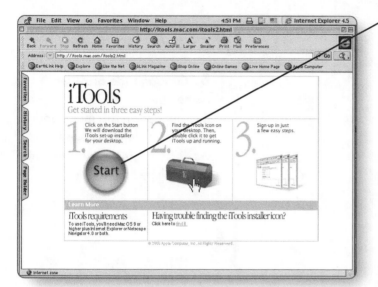

5. Click on **Start**. The iTools installer icon will download to your desktop.

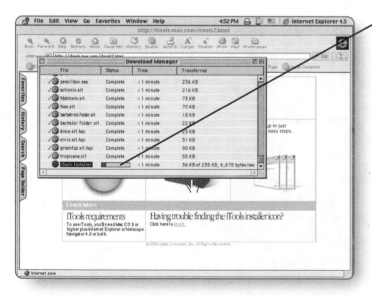

6. Wait for the **installer** to finish downloading. The iTools installer icon will appear on your desktop when it's finished downloading.

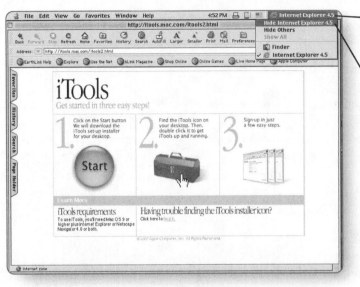

7. Click on the **Finder**. The Finder menu will appear.

8. Click on **Hide *browser name*** (the name of the browser that appears in this menu option depends on which browser and version you are using). The Web page will be hidden.

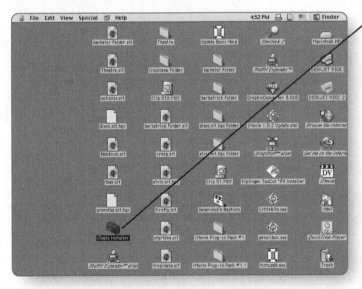

9. Locate and **double-click** on the **iTools Installer** (it looks like a red toolbox). The iTools New Member Sign Up page will appear.

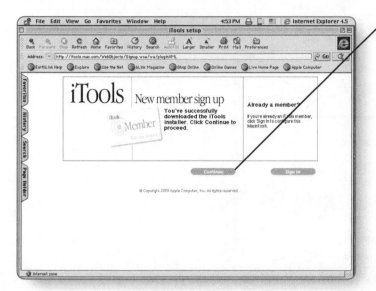

10. Click on **Continue**. The iTools Select your country page will appear.

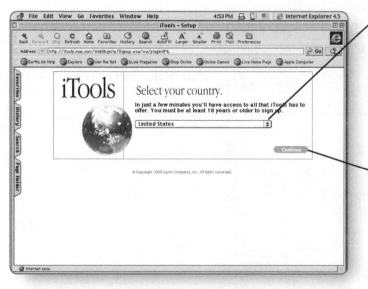

11. Click on the **up and down arrows** to the right of the list box. A drop-down list will appear.

12. Click on your **country**. Your country will be selected.

13. Click on **Continue**. The iTools Tell us about yourself page will appear.

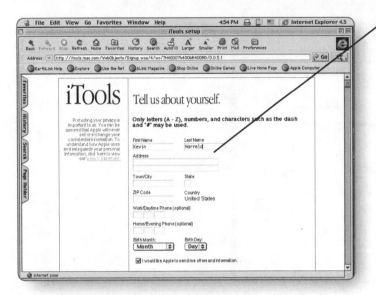

14. Fill in the **text boxes** with the appropriate information about yourself.

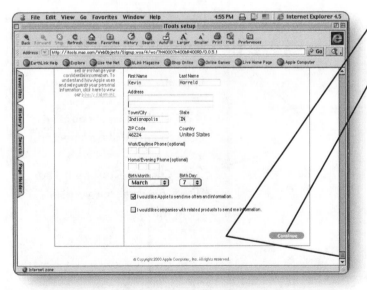

15. **Scroll** down to the **bottom** of the page.

16. **Click** on **Continue**. The Terms of Agreement page will appear.

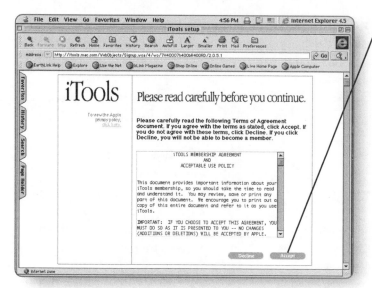

17. Read the **membership agreement terms** and **click** on **Accept** if you agree to these terms. The Choose your member name and password page will appear.

18. Type a **member name** in the Member Name text box.

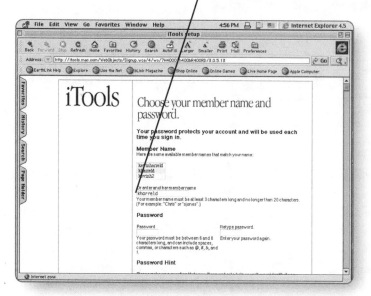

NOTE

iTools might provide some sample member names for you. If you like one of them, click on it, and it will appear in the Member Name text box.

19. **Type** a **password** in the Password text box. The password will appear as a series of dots rather than the actual characters you type.

20. **Retype** the **password** in the Retype password text box.

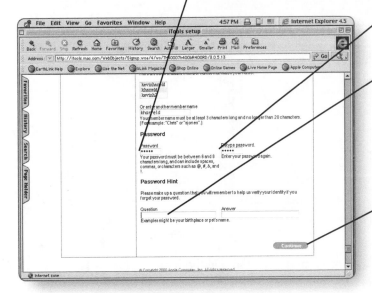

21. **Type** a **Question and Answer** in the appropriate Password Hint text boxes. This will help Apple identify you if you forget your password and need to be reminded of it.

22. **Click** on **Continue**. The iTools Save for your records page will appear. This page contains your member name, password, and newly assigned e-mail address.

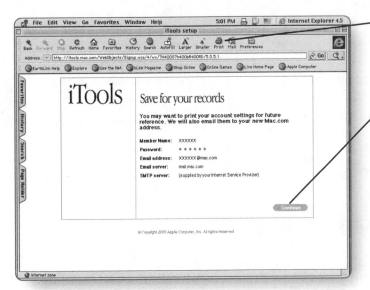

23. **Click** on the **Print button**. You will want to keep this info for your records, in case you ever need to access it.

24. **Click** on **Continue**. You will be taken to the Announce your new email address page. From here, you can send cards to your friends announcing your new address (if you choose to use the address).

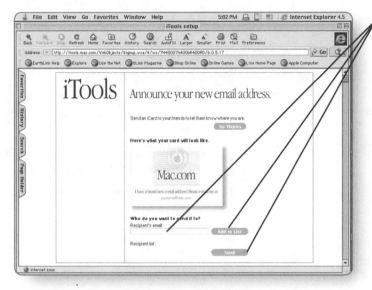

25a. Type the **e-mail address** of one of your friends or family members in the Recipient's email text box and **click** on **Add to List**. The name will be added to the recipient list beneath the text box. **Repeat this step** for every person to whom you wish to announce your address. When you are finished compiling the list, **click** on **Send**. An electronic postcard announcing your e-mail address will be sent to every person on your recipient list, and you will be taken to the Member sign in page.

OR

25b. Click on **No Thanks** if you don't want to send out this address information. You will then be taken to the Member sign in page.

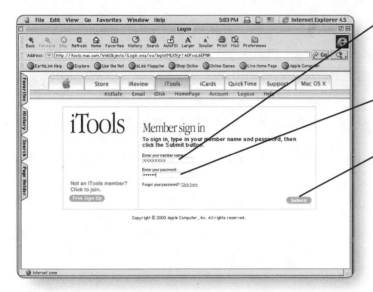

26. Type your **member name** in the Enter your member name text box.

27. Type your **password** in the Enter your password text box.

28. Click on **Submit**. You are now an official iTools member, with access to all of the perks.

When you sign in, notice that the iTools opening page includes Go buttons in the Email, KidSafe, iDisk, and HomePage areas. Now that you are a member, you can access all of these services by clicking on their respective Go buttons.

Accessing Your iDisk

Before you create your Web site to premiere your iMovies, you need to open iDisk. iDisk creates 20 MB of storage space for you on Apple's Internet server. It basically works as a backup disk of free and secure storage. It is also the avenue through which you import your iMovies (compressed into QuickTime movies, of course) into your soon-to-be-created Web site. iTools will not allow you to post an iMovie on your Web site without first importing it into iDisk.

1. From the iTools opening page, **click** on the **Go** at the bottom of the iDisk section. The iDisk page will appear.

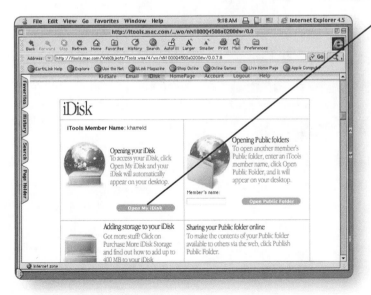

2. Click on **Open My iDisk**. After a minute or so, the iDisk icon will appear on your desktop.

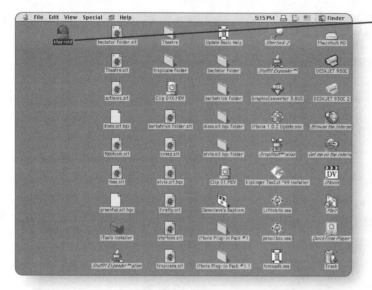

3. Double-click on the **iDisk icon**. Your iDisk window will open and will have your member name in the title bar.

4. Open the **folder** on your hard drive that contains the QuickTime movie you want to post on your site.

The folder will open.

5. Press and hold the **mouse button** on the QuickTime movie and **drag** the **movie** to the Movies folder in the iDisk window.

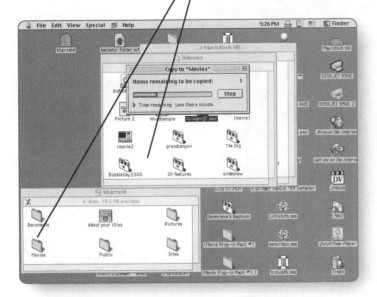

6. Release the **mouse button**. The movie will transfer to the iDisk. Depending on the size of the movie, this could take several minutes.

7. Click on the **Finder**. The Finder menu will appear.

8. Click on the **name of your browser**. You will return to the iTools page. You now have access to iDisk, a free and safe storage haven that is like an extra hard drive, and it includes a movie that is ready to be posted on your home page, which you will create in the next section.

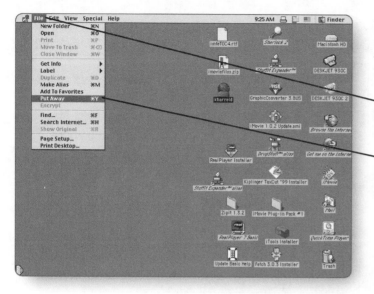

9. To exit iTools, **click** on the **iDisk icon** on your desktop. The icon will be selected.

10. Click on **File**. The File menu will appear.

11. Click on **Put Away**. Your iTools account will be closed.

Creating and Editing Your Home Page

Now you are ready to create the online forum where you can showcase the iMovie that you spent hours filming, editing, and polishing. Apple makes it simple to create this iMovie theater on your Web site by providing templates that are designed especially for iMovie posting. After you create this Web page, feel free to use the other Web page templates that Apple offers (birth announcements and photo albums, for example) and add them to your site.

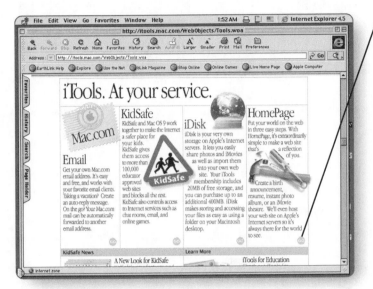

1. From the iTools opening page, **click** on the **Go** at the bottom of the HomePage section. (If you are still on the iDisk page, click on the Back button in your browser until you reach the iTools page again.) The HomePage main page will appear.

2. Click on **iMovies** in the Create A Page section. Four themes will appear to the right: Theater, Retro-TV, iMovie Kids, and Drive-In.

3. Click on a **theme**. The theme will be selected and your dummy page will appear.

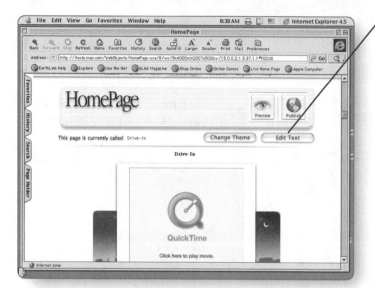

4. Click on **Edit Text**. Text boxes will appear for you to add a page title, movie title, and movie description.

5. Select the **placeholder text** and **type** the **title** for your page.

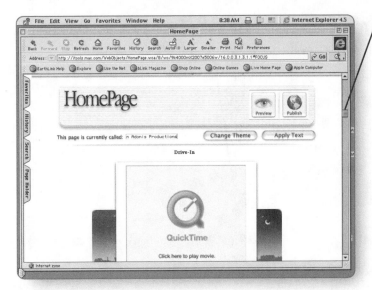

6. Scroll down to the **bottom** of the page.

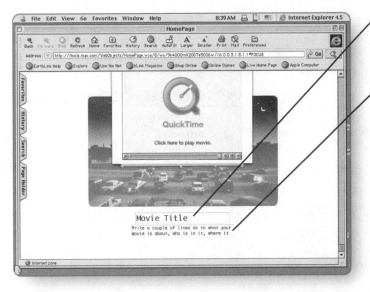

7. Select the **placeholder text** and **type** a **title** for the movie you plan to post.

8. Select the **placeholder text** and **type** a **description** for your movie.

9. Scroll back up to the top of the page.

10. Click on **Apply Text**. All of the text you typed will be applied to your page.

11. Click on **Edit Text** to make any changes to the text you just entered.

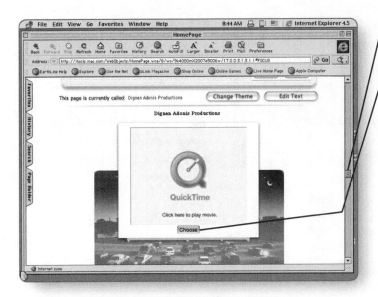

12. Scroll down to the **middle** of the page.

13. Click on **Choose** under the QuickTime icon. The Choose an iMovie page will appear.

14. Click on the **movie** that you added to your iDisk in the list box on the left side of the page. The movie will be selected.

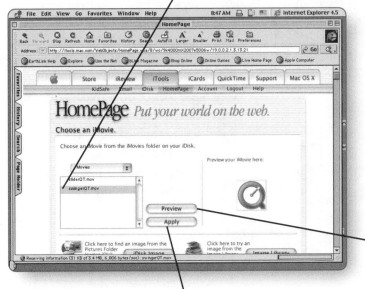

NOTE

This iTools page refers to your movies as iMovies, but what they mean are your iMovies compressed into QuickTime movies. So again, make sure you are importing compressed QuickTime versions of your iMovies.

15. Click on **Preview** if you want to see a preview of your movie. The movie will play in the box on the right.

16. Click on **Apply**. The movie will be added to your Web page, and you will return to the HomePage main page.

17. Click on **Click here to play movie** under the QuickTime icon. It may take a few minutes for the iMovie file to upload.

18. Click on **Preview**. The movie will play, and you will see the page as it will appear after it is published.

19. After viewing the page, **click** on **Edit** if you want to make edits to the text or titles, or to change the movie on your page.

20. Click on **Publish** if you are happy with your page. The page will be published to the Web, and you will see a Congratulations page that displays the address of your page.

21. **Click** on the **link** to go to your Web page. You will be taken to your page.

22. **Click** on the **Back button** in your browser. You will return to the Congratulations page.

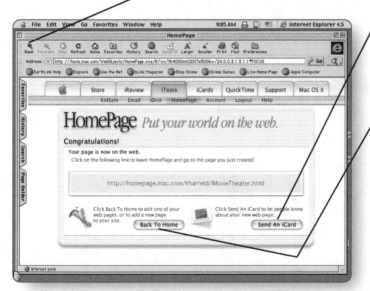

23. Optionally, **click** on the **Send An iCard** to send e-mail messages to friends announcing your new Web site.

24. **Click** on **Back To Home** to make changes to this page or to add more pages to your Web site. The page that you just created will appear in the list box on the left.

25. **Click** on the **name of the page** you just created. The page will be selected.

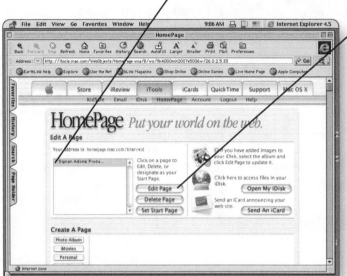

26. **Click** on **Edit Page or Delete Page** to edit or delete the selected page, respectively.

NOTE

To designate the selected page as the start page of your Web site, click on Set Start Page. You can also create another page for your Web site from this page by moving to the Create A Page section.

27. **Click** on **Logout** on the iTools toolbar when you are finished working in iTools. You will return to the Apple home page.

Part IV Review Questions

1. What still image file formats are compatible with iMovie 2? *See Extracting Still Images from Your Videos in Chapter 11*

2. How do you save a moment from your video as a still? *See Creating a Still Image within Your iMovie Project in Chapter 11*

3. How do you import a photo into your iMovie project? *See Adding a Still Image to an iMovie in Chapter 11*

4. What other programs can you use to enhance text in iMovie 2? *See the introduction in Chapter 12*

5. How can you add more excitement to your text in iMovie 2? *See Chapter 12*

6. What are the benefits of an iTools account? *See Setting up an iTools Account in Chapter 13*

7. What's so special about iDisk? *See Accessing Your iDisk in Chapter 13*

8. Why do you need to open iDisk before importing a movie to your Web site? *See Accessing Your iDisk in Chapter 13*

9. What format does your iMovie have to be in to post it on your Web site? *See Accessing Your iDisk in Chapter 13*

10. How much free space do you have to use on your home page? *See Accessing Your iDisk in Chapter 13*

PART V

Appendixes

A

Acquiring and Installing iMovie 2

Downloading and installing iMovie 2 from Apple's Web site is a fairly simple task. If you don't have iMovie 2 already installed on your machine, you can purchase the download version from Apple for $49. The download version does not include the tutorial files, and iMovie 2 is not available in a CD-ROM version. You will need an Internet connection and a small amount of free time. In this appendix, you'll learn how to:

- Acquire iMovie 2
- Install iMovie 2
- Update iMovie 2

Acquiring iMovie 2

1. Go to **Apple's iMovie Web page** (http://www.apple.com/ imovie). You will see a page introducing iMovie 2.

2. Click on the **Download iMovie 2 icon**. The Review Your Order page will appear with your order.

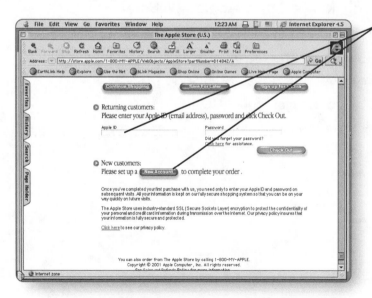

3. If you have an Apple ID, **enter it** in the box provided. Otherwise, **click** on **New Account** to create a new account. The Account Profile page will appear.

4. Type your **personal information** in the boxes.

5. Click on **Continue**. The Shipping Info page will appear.

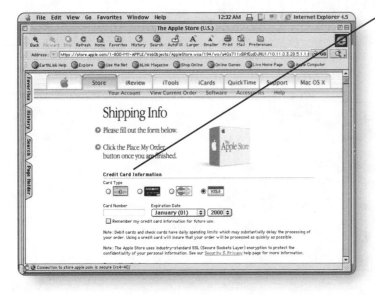

6. Type your **credit card information** in the boxes.

7. Click on **Place My Order**. Your order will be placed and the iMovie download page will appear.

8. Click on the **Download iMovie 2 link**. If Internet Explorer is your browser, the Download Manager will appear, showing you the progress of the download. You can sit back and relax, because it will take a while.

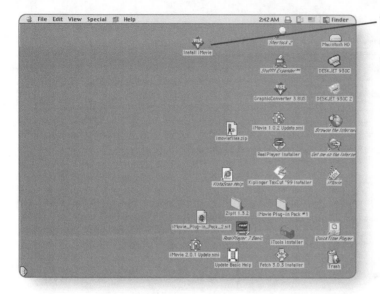

When the download is complete, an Install iMovie icon will appear on your desktop.

Installing iMovie 2

If you have a previous version of iMovie installed on your machine, you must first drag that version to the trash before installing the new version.

1. **Double-click** on the **Install iMovie icon**. An iMovie program icon will appear on your desktop, and the iMovie window containing the Install iMovie icon and Read Me files will open.

2. **Double-click** on the **Install iMovie icon**. The Install iMovie dialog box will open.

3. **Click** on **Continue**. The License Agreement Page will open.

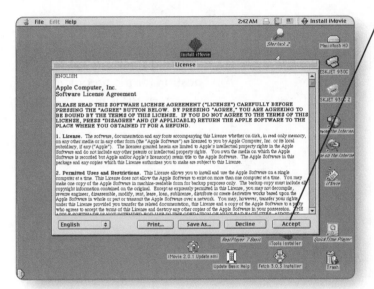

4. Click on **Accept**. The Read Me page will open.

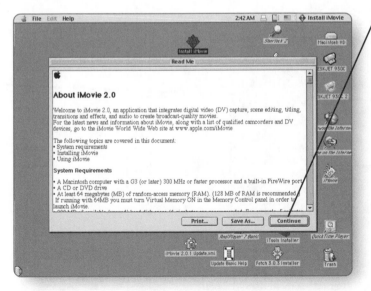

5. Click on **Continue**. The Install iMovie window will appear.

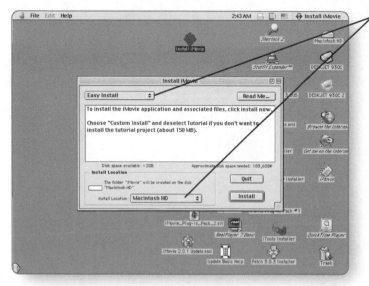

6. Make sure **Easy Install** is **selected** in the top-left pop-up menu and **select** an **Install Location** for the program (Macintosh HD is the recommended location). Then, **click** on **Install**. iMovie will proceed to install on your hard drive.

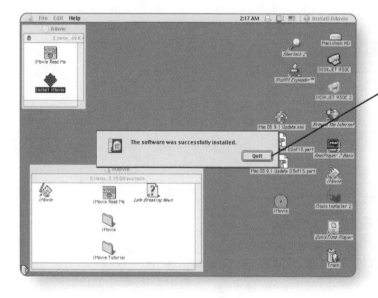

A message box will appear, letting you know that the installation has finished.

7. **Click** on **Quit**. The message box will disappear.

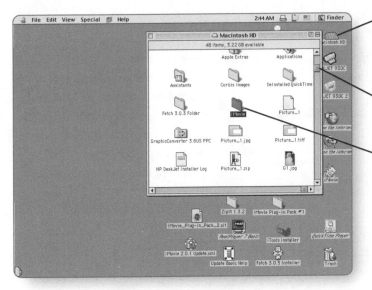

8. **Double-click** on your **hard drive icon**. The hard drive window will open.

9. **Click** on the **scroll bar** to find the iMovie folder.

10. **Double-click** on the **iMovie folder**. The iMovie folder will open.

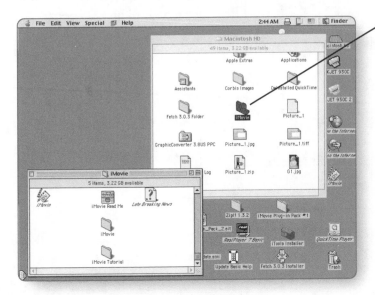

11. **Double-click** on the **iMovie icon**. The program will open, and you can begin using iMovie.

Updating iMovie 2

Apple provides an update to iMovie 2 that, once installed, will allow you to take advantage of additional special effects, transitions, and title plug-ins. (See Chapter 6, "Adding Stylish Transitions," to read about acquiring this plug-in pack.) iMovie 2 must be updated to version 2.0.1 in order to use these special plug-ins.

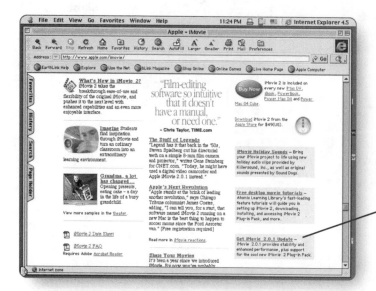

1. Navigate to the **iMovie page** on Apple's Web site.

2. Click on the **Get iMovie 2.0.1 Update link**. The Software Downloads page will appear.

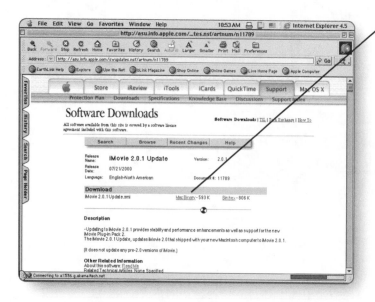

3. Click on the **MacBinary link** in the Download section. The update will download to your desktop.

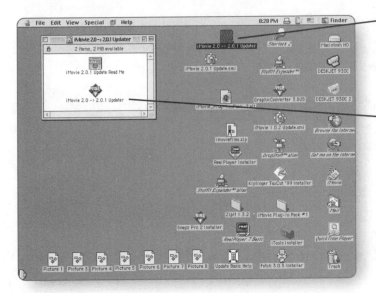

4. **Double-click** on the **compressed Updater icon** on your desktop. The updater will uncompress to your desktop.

5. **Double-click** on the **Updater icon**. The first page of the updater will open.

6. **Click** on **Continue**. The License Agreement will appear.

7. **Click** on **Accept**. The Updater page will appear.

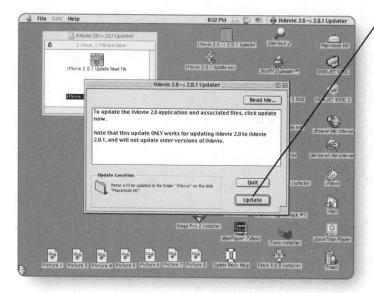

8. **Click** on **Update**. The update will install.

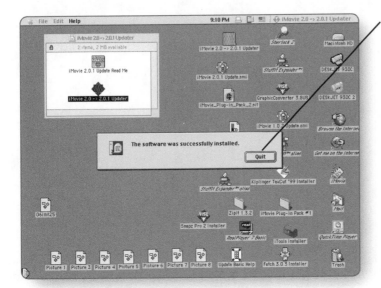

9. Click on **Quit** when the install is finished. iMovie will be updated.

B

iMovie 2 Keyboard Shortcuts

There are numerous keyboard shortcuts available in iMovie. Shortcuts for menu functions and navigation make using iMovie even easier.

File Menu Functions

Action	Shortcut
New Project	Command + N
Open Project	Command + O
Save Project	Command + S
Export Movie	Command + E
Save Frame As	Command + F
Import File	Command + I
Quit	Command + Q

Edit Menu Functions

Action	Shortcut
Undo	Command + Z
Redo	Shift + Command + Z
Cut	Command + X
Copy	Command + C
Paste	Command + V
Crop	Command + K
Split Clip at Playhead	Command + T
Select All	Command + A
Select None	Command + D

Navigation Shortcuts

Action	Shortcut
Play/Stop and Start/Stop capture	Space bar
Playhead to beginning of movie	Home
Playhead to end of movie	End
Forward one frame	Right arrow
Forward 10 frames	Shift + right arrow
Fast forward	Command +]
Back one frame	Left arrow
Back 10 frames	Shift + Left arrow
Rewind	Command + [

Selection Shortcuts

Action	Shortcut
Multiple selection	Shift + Click items
Range of selection	Click first item, then Shift + click last item in range

Moving and Cropping Shortcuts

Action	Shortcut
Move audio clip	Click clip + left or right arrow
Move audio clip 10 frames	Click clip, then Shift + left or right arrow
Move crop marker	Click marker, then Shift + left or right arrow

Glossary

AIFF audio file. Audio Interchange File Format. A digital audio file that can be used in iMovie.

Alignment. The position of the text in your iMovie project.

Analog video. Common video formats such as VHS, SVHS, 8mm, and Hi8.

Browser. A program designed for viewing Web pages on the Internet.

Clip. A media file that contains audio, video, or still images.

Clipboard. Temporary storage containing the last item you copied in iMovie.

Clip Viewer. A timeline that displays your video clips, titles, and transitions. It is located at the bottom of the screen, along with the Timeline Viewer, and has an eye icon on the tab.

Close-up shot. A zoomed-in, tight frame of an object or subject.

Compression. Reducing the data size of a file.

Copy. A command that takes a video or audio clip and duplicates it on the Clipboard.

Crop. A process that cuts the unwanted video or audio from the beginning and/or end of a clip.

Cut. A command that takes a video or audio clip and moves it to the Clipboard, removing it from the iMovie project.

Download. To copy a file or application from the Internet.

DV. Digital video format. DV stores video and audio information as data in a digital form.

Edit. To assemble your movie by cutting, rearranging, altering, and refining your video and audio clips.

Export. A command used to convert your iMovie files into another format, such as QuickTime or digital or analog videotape.

File. Information stored on a single disk under one name.

File format. A generic term for describing the way a file is saved. JPEG, PICT, and AIFF are different types of graphic and audio file formats.

Filter. Programs such as Photoshop and QuickTime Pro include image-editing filters to adjust contrast and brightness and add other types of special effects to improve your video images.

FireWire. Apple Computer's multimedia peripheral that allows you to import and export video and audio from your camcorder at tremendous speeds. Also known as iLink or IEEE 1394.

Folder. An organizational tool used to store files.

Font. A character set of a specific typeface, type style, and type size. Some fonts are installed with the operating system on your computer.

Frame. A single image from a video clip.

Frame rate. The number of frames per second displayed onscreen.

Full shot. A video shot that gives the audience the setting of the scene and establishes how the subject of your movie fits in with the background or surroundings.

Hard disk. A hardware component on which you can store files and folders of data.

Help. A feature that gives you additional information and instructions about iMovie 2.

Image. A bitmapped matrix of pixels that represents a picture.

Import. A command used to convert digital video, still images, and audio files in iMovie 2.

JPEG. Joint Photographic Experts Group. Compresses images into smaller file sizes. This format is mostly used in still image files sent as e-mail attachments or used on the Web.

Kilobyte. Commonly referred to as KB. Equivalent to 1,024 bytes.

Lock Audio. A feature that allows you to lock your audio clip to a video clip. When you move a clip in the Timeline, the audio will move with it.

Media. All of your files, including images, sounds, music, and stills.

Medium shot. A video shot that shows one to three players within a small area, including their gestures and expressions.

Megabyte. Commonly referred to as MB. Equivalent to 1,048,576 bytes.

Memory. Also known as RAM. Refers to the amount of physical memory in your computer. Virtual memory is the amount of memory or hard disk space allocated for use by the operating system and applications on a computer. In regard to iMovie, memory represents the amount of space required for the program to run.

Menu. A user-interface element originating from the operating system, containing commands for an application.

Mode switch. Buttons under the Monitor window that allow you to switch between Camera and Edit modes.

Monitor window. The large preview area located in the top-left corner of your iMovie screen. Includes playback controls, volume control, and a Scrubber bar.

Narration. Using your voice as a storytelling effect in your movies.

Pan. Rotating the video camera slowly and steadily along a horizontal line from right to left, or vice versa.

Paste. The process of retrieving the information stored on the Clipboard and inserting it into your project.

PICT. Macintosh picture file format. Doesn't compress an image; therefore, the image maintains the same quality when it is copied.

Playback controls. The Play, Fast Forward, Rewind, Play Full-Screen, and Home controls under the Monitor window.

Play Full-Screen button. A button in the Monitor window, located next to the Play button, that allows you to view your movie on the entire computer screen.

Playhead. The small triangular icon in the Scrubber bar. Indicates the starting point of video or audio clip playback or recording.

Preview. A feature in iMovie that enables you to see what a title, transition, frame, or completed movie will look like before you render or save it.

Processor. The central processing unit of a computer. A faster processor will run iMovie faster than a slower processor.

RAM. See *Memory*.

Rendering. Adding elements together (for example, adding text to a clip or transitions between clips) to change the visual information on a frame of video.

Resolution. The number of horizontal and vertical pixels that make up a screen of information.

Restore. A button that allows you to restore captured clips to their original length after you've made a crop.

Save. A command used to convert your iMovie projects stored in memory into files.

Scroll bar. A set of window controls consisting of up and down and left and right arrows, a scroll button, and a scroll bar that can be used to navigate a document window.

Scrolling Shelf. The warehouse, in the upper-right portion of the iMovie 2 screen, where your video clips are temporarily stored.

Scrubber bar. The bar used to position the playhead; it is located under the Monitor window and in the Timeline Viewer.

Size. The file size of a document. iMovie files are very large, eating up several MBs of hard disk space on your computer.

Submenu. Also known as a cascading menu. A secondary menu containing a list of menu commands.

Timeline. Houses the Clip Viewer and the Timeline Viewer, located at the bottom of the screen. This is where you create your movie.

Timeline Viewer. It is located at the bottom of the screen, along with the Clip Viewer, and has a clock icon on the tab. Add music and sound effects, or edit audio clips on this tab.

Transition. The effect of blending or smoothing out the cut between two separate video frames.

Trash can. Where you drag your unwanted clips to delete them from your movie and free up hard disk space on your computer.

Undo. A menu command that enables you to reverse a previous action you made in the document window.

Viewer. The timeline at the bottom of your iMovie screen. Includes the Clip Viewer for editing and viewing DV clips, and the Timeline Viewer for editing music, narration, and sound effects.

Web. The World Wide Web. A group of computers running Web server software, connected to an extended network around the world.

Zoom. To slowly move toward or away from the subject in your video.

Index